The Oracles of God

Exploring God's Wisdom About Life: The Unfamiliar and the Spiritual

The Oracles of God

Exploring God's Wisdom About Life: The Unfamiliar and the Spiritual

Richard Wurmbrand

Destiny Image Publishers
P.O. Box 310
Shippensburg, PA 17257

"Speaking to the Purposes of God for this Generation
and for the Generations to Come"

ISBN 1-56043-143-1

For Worldwide Distribution
Printed in the U.S.A.

Destiny Image books are available through these fine distributors outside the United States:

Christian Growth, Inc.
Jalan Kilang-Timor, Singapore 0315

Successful Christian Living
Capetown, Rep. of South Africa

Lifestream
Nottingham, England

Vision Resources
Ponsonby, Auckland, New Zealand

Rhema Ministries Trading
Randburg, South Africa

WA Buchanan Company
Geebung, Queensland, Australia

Salvation Book Centre
Petaling, Jaya, Malaysia

Word Alive
Niverville, Manitoba, Canada

Inside the U.S., call toll free to order:
1-800-722-6774

Contents

Books by
Richard Wurmbrand

The Overcomers
From Suffering to Triumph
The Answer to the Atheist's Handbook
Christ on the Jewish Road
Reaching Towards the Heights
The Sweetest Song
With God in Solitary Confinement
Tortured for Christ
From the Lips of Children
My Correspondence With Jesus
In God's Underground
Alone With God
If Prison Walls Could Speak
and others

A list of addresses is included in the back of this book for your convenience in contacting the author.

About the Author

In 1992, *70 Great Christians Changing the World* by Geoffrey Hanks appeared in Great Britian (Christian Focus Publication). Peter and Paul, Apostles; Ignatius, Polycarp, martyrs of old; St. Jerome, Augustine, Columbus, world renowned teachers; Patrick, apostle of the Irish; Francis of Assisi, Wyclif, Luther, Tyndale, Bible translators; John Knoxx, Scottish reformer; Luther and Ignatius of Loyala, Carey (the father of modern missions); Hudson Taylor, Livingstone, founders of missions in Asia and Africa; Barnardo, founder of orphanages; William Booth, founder of the Salvation Army; Spurgeon and Moody, two of the greatest evangelic preachers ever; and other people like these are listed in this book. Included in this book is a chapter on Richard Wurmbrand. He is counted among the 70 greatest Christians our world has known.

This listing in Hank's book tops all other reports of Wurmbrand, both good and bad, that have been recorded in the world press. The following is a selection of some of these.

"Wurmbrand irritates, but he opens our eyes...Wurmbrand has gotten the world to hearken, even if he has sacrificed himself. He has reached quite a bit...Wurmbrand has shouted the cry of the martyrs."

The Rev. Ingemar Martinson
General Secretary of the Slavic Mission
Sweden

"Wurmbrand is an Iron Curtain Paul. He is the most authoritative voice of the Underground Church, he is more than a living martyr."

Underground Evangelism

"Since the Sermon on the Mount was delivered, no one has preached with love like Richard Wurmbrand."

Haratta
Finland

"Wurmbrand has brought to the universal Church a new dimension, reminding it about the martyrs."

Church Times
London

"Wurmbrand burst like a fireball across the cool complacency of some."

USA Congressional Record

"We were hit by a hurricane call Wurmbrand."
Tablet,
New Zealand

"We have checked and can say with almost certainty that there has never been a Pastor Wurmbrand in Romania."
Finnish Communist newspaper

"In the present Communist regimes strong powers for the humanization of society lie hidden...Wurmbrand becomes really dangerous."
Van deHeuwell
(while Director of Public Relations
The World Council of Churches)

"Wurmbrand is the devil's mouthpiece."
Arbeiterzeitung
Switzerland

"Wurmbrand is a new St. John the Baptist...a voice crying in the wilderness."
Christianity Today
USA

"Wurmbrand is a passionate anti-Communist and anti-Soviet. His books are full of unveiled hatred.
several Soviet newspapers

"Except for the Bible, nothing has shaken me like Wurmbrand's *Tortured for Christ.* It is the message of the century. Even more: since the persecution of

Christians by Nero, it is the most powerful Act of Martyrs."

Dr. Kurt Koch
renowned German evangelical
pastor and author

"Wurmbrand is broadly charitable in his understanding of God's love and the nature of man. Not even an ounce of contentiousness appears in his books. Perhaps the agony of long imprisonment purges that out of a man.

Alliance Witness
USA

"Wurmbrand is a dirty Jew."

Christian Vanguard
USA

"What I have to say about myself is much simpler: I am an ordinary Christian who lived in very unusual circumstances."

Richard Wurmbrand

Prologue

The Rev. Richard Wurmbrand is an evangelical minister of Jewish descent. Most of his family members died in the Holocaust. He endured more than fourteen years of Fascist and Communist imprisonment and torture in his homeland of Romania. He is one of Romania's most widely known Christian leaders, authors, and educators.

In 1945, when Soviet troops invaded Romania and the new Communist regime attempted to control the churches for its own purposes, Richard Wurmbrand immediately began an effective, vigorous "underground" ministry to his enslaved people and to the Russian soldiers. He was finally arrested in 1948, along with his wife Sabina. Sabina served three years as a slave-laborer. Richard Wurmbrand spent three years in solitary confinement—seeing no one but his Communist torturers. Following this period, he was transferred to a mass cell for five years. There the torture continued.

Due to his international stature as a Christian leader, diplomats of foreign embassies made inquiries about his safety to the Communist government. They were told he had fled Romania. Secret police, posing as released fellow-prisoners, told his wife stories of attending his burial in the prison cemetery. His family in Romania and his friends abroad were all told to forget him since he was now dead. After spending eight years in prison, Rev. Wurmbrand was released. He promptly resumed his work with the underground Church. Two years later, in 1959, he was re-arrested and sentenced to 25 years in prison.

Rev. Wurmbrand was released in a general amnesty in 1964, and again he continued his underground ministry. Realizing the great danger of a third imprisonment, Christians in Norway negotiated with the Communist authorities for his release from Romania; the Communist government had begun "selling" its political prisoners. The "going price" for a prisoner was set at $1,900, but the price for Wurmbrand was $10,000.

In May 1966, Richard Wurmbrand testified in Washington, D.C. before the Senate's Internal Security Subcommittee. He stripped to the waist to show eighteen deep torture wounds covering his body. His story was carried across the world in newspapers throughout the U.S., Europe, and Asia. In September 1966, Wurmbrand was warned that the Romanian Communist regime had made a decision to assassinate him, yet even in the face of these threats, he refused to be silent. He has been called the "voice of the Underground Church." Christian leaders have referred to him as a "living martyr" and the "Iron Curtain Paul."

In October 1967, Richard and Sabina Wurmbrand founded a non-profit missionary organization to bring assistance to persecuted Christians around the world. Today, **The Voice of the Martyrs, Inc.**, directed by Pastor Wurmbrand, continues to carry out this work.

Preface

*If anyone speaks, let him speak **as the oracles of God**...* (1 Peter 4:11).

Did you ever meet a person who speaks *as the oracles of God*? Do you speak like this? If not, why not? If this Scripture is from God, every bit of speech that is not spoken as His oracle is grave sin. Oracles was a name given to certain priestesses or priests in heathen religions of the past through which sure revelations were given.

How does one arrive at speaking like an oracle? This is the subject of the present book. Would it seem presumptuous to you if I would say that I speak as an oracle of God? But why would a Christian dare to write a book if he would not be convinced of this?

I am not bound to think and write only about dictatorships and jails, nor only about missionary practices. This time I wrote a book with the thoughts about God and human life.

I had most of these thoughts when I was alone in a solitary cell, 30 feet beneath the earth, never, but never, seeing sun, moon, stars, trees, flowers, birds, butterflies. I never saw any other color than gray— the gray of the walls and of our prison uniform. I never heard a voice except the insults of those who watched us.

Don't wonder if some of these thoughts will seem strange.

The same One who said, "Don't murder, don't steal," said, "Speak as my oracles." Ponder about this.

Pastor Richard Wurmbrand

Introduction

A soldier in need approached Alexander the Great and asked for some money. The emperor, who knew the bravery of this soldier in battle, refused, but instead made him ruler over one of his cities. Overcome by such royal largesse, the soldier demurred, exclaiming, "This gift is too big for me!"

"That may be," responded the emperor. "But it is not too great a gift on the part of a king."

As you begin to read this book, you anticipate another collection of human thoughts to be found within its covers. It is proper for you to not ask for much. But I write in the name of Christ, for whom it is customary to give more than a man usually expects. He is the King of Kings. *When one writes in His name or speaks on His behalf, he is expected to speak the oracles of God* (see 1 Pet. 4:11).

Shakespeare might have meant just such a man when he wrote:

"His words are bonds, his oaths are oracles.
His love sincere, his thoughts immaculate,
His tears pure messages, sent from his heart,
His heart as far from fraud, as heaven from
earth."

In mystery religions of old (as in the Lamaists' religion of today), some priests or priestesses were put into a trance-like state through drugs, dances, or incense, and what they spoke in this condition was thought to come from their god and was therefore deemed an "oracle."

The one who writes or preaches in the name of Christ is meant to be God-intoxicated, a person who has first received the kiss of God.

For not savoring the mind of God, the Lord once reproached Peter: "...You are not mindful of the things of God, but the things of men" (Mt. 16:23).

Any man who deals with religious matters, not only the apostles, should not open his mouth unless what he says is a revelation from God. It might be but a little drop from the sea, but it must still be from the sea itself. His words must savor of the things of God.

The Hebrew language has strange expressions for our terms "to speak" or "to tell"; we consider every word expressed, however foolish, as falling into the category of "speaking," not so the Jews. It is in their genius to believe that the word is divine. For "to speak" they use *ledaber*, akin to *davar*, which is used for word. But *davar* is also the word for "thing." Hebrew words are real things, not simply talk. *Ledaber* means "to communicate a reality."

Another word for "to speak" is *le-omer*, from the root *amir*, which means the highest branch of a tree. A man's words are worthy only if he speaks at the highest level he can reach.

For "to tell," the word is *le-saper*, from *saper* meaning "sapphire." "To tell" is to give another a jewel. If you have a jewel to give, talk. If not, keep silent.

It is a risky thing for an author to write a book such as this, but I do so because I love you, my reader.

This book, then, contains the oracles of God.

* * *

Some readers may already be laughing skeptically: "What an absurd claim, to speak the oracles of God!" Countless men throughout the ages have claimed to speak such oracles and some still do. All the false prophets and messiahs among the Jewish people, founders of new religions like Mohammed and of new sects like Joseph Smith and Mary Baker Eddy not only claimed, but sincerely believed, that they spoke the oracles of God. All the promoters of heresies have done so, as did the inquisitors. Hitler and Khomeini spoke as if they were voices of Providence.

So why do I make such a claim?

Well, if you have already begun to laugh, I will tell you a joke to make you laugh even more.

A man named George wanted to sell his horse and therefore boasted among his acquaintances, "My horse is indeed unique. In the morning I send him to the baker and to the dairy, and he brings me bread and milk, as well as the newspaper. The horse knows the way from my home to the office and back. I give him free rein in the evening, and he takes me to my club."

Tom was deeply impressed and paid $2,000 to obtain this remarkable horse.

After much time had passed, George and Tom met at a party. Tom immediately launched into a dismal recital of the horse's inadequacies: "It only likes to enjoy itself, and it is lazy and stubborn when you want to saddle it up for a ride. It doesn't understand any of the things I want it to do."

George warned Tom, "Stop talking like that or you won't be able to sell the horse. I got a good price because I praised it!"

Obviously, only highly touted political and religious convictions are accepted by the populace. Anyone who wants to propagate an idea must boast of its merits. Every salesman for a product has to claim that it is the best.

But one idea, one product, is *really* the best. The idea of a "best product" cannot be discarded simply because lesser products are also touted as "top of the line."

Of the many pretended oracles of God, some are genuine, some false. It is up to you to determine whether or not what I write is indeed a genuine sapphire.

Every book on metaphysical or religious matters will be useless or even harmful if the reader does not have the gift of a discerning spirit. He must be able to find out if what is presented to him is actually a message from God.

If a book only amuses, then enjoy it and have a little fun. If it claims to be from God but does not contain a message from Him, don't waste time on it. If it does, then you are obliged to accept its ideas in a spirit of obedience. The Master speaks through the author, and you will have to fulfill what He says.

When a reader seeking treasure encounters a writer with jewels to share, amazing things can happen. But the character and frame of mind of the reader must be part of the equation. Then if the writer speaks truth, the reader can expect sure and salutary results.

But be very sure about the writer. Ask yourself whether God speaks through him to your soul, whether the devil speaks, or if this is some human being merely expressing his own thoughts. Most readers, or listeners, are remarkably inattentive.

An experiment was carried out in Israel. The well-known radio announcer Kishon read a novel on the radio, beginning with the last chapter and ending with the first. Then he read only the odd pages of another novel. Later he announced a novel and read the State budget. Only one man was moved to complain.

People swallow bad books, bad sermons, and bad lectures with the same ease with which they swallow good ones—I would even say with greater ease.

Only if you are wary can the reading of this book be of value to you.

* * *

I present this book with the claim that it contains an important message.

What God has for you in this book is not an ordinary gift. Earthly gifts may provide great pleasure, but ultimately they are vain.

In Iran, near the town of Shiraz, there is a small, simple tomb with this inscription: "Man, whosoever you are, and whenever you will come, because I know that you will come, I tell you that I am Emperor Cyrus and that I conquered for the Persians the dominion of the world. Leave me at least with this little piece of land that covers my body." This minimal request has not been fulfilled; his tomb has been depredated.

The earthly gifts God provides are temporary. In time, wicked men or the forces of nature will take them from us. He gives us earthly gifts while making it clear from the beginning they are but tokens that should open our hearts to receive the one great eternal gift reserved for us. This gift is what this book is all about.

I wonder how many of you have ever played cards. If you have, you know that it is neither advantageous nor fun to play with open cards. The challenge and enjoyment lie in *not knowing* another's cards, in guessing and surmising which cards your opponent may hold. God keeps man in suspense; man doesn't know what trump cards God is holding. An author representing God through his books must do likewise.

I do not want to tell you what God's gift is until I have prepared your heart to receive it. I want to awaken within you a state of intense desire for the unknown and the invisible. I put all my soul into what I write.

Chapter 1

Possess the Truth

A perceptive child can often spot insincerity or indifference. In Sunday school, when the teacher recounted the story of Jesus' sufferings and death, a child remarked, "The story is not true."

Taken aback, the teacher asked, "What makes you say that?"

"If it were true," the boy replied quietly, "you could not tell it without weeping."

Sorrily, some Christian writers, authors of religious hymns, and preachers are boring; others are very good but burn out quickly; and some become soul-less—perhaps it is because they spend too much of their souls on their work without taking due precautions to refill them daily.

William Cowper wrote the renowned hymn:

"There is a fountain, filled with blood,
Drawn from Emmanuel's veins,

And sinners plunged beneath that flood
Lose all their guilty stains.
The dying thief rejoiced to see
That fountain in his day,
And there may I, though vile as he,
Wash all my sins away."

One feels there is life in this song. Cowper poured into it the blood of his own heart. In his old age, he suffered several bouts of insanity; he who had written that "the precious blood shall never lose its power" doubted during his depressions that his own sins were washed away by Christ's sacrifice.

It is necessary that we allow ourselves to be cleansed and purified.

To be in error is a dreadful thing, but it is even worse to embrace truth for the wrong reasons: because it is convenient, because it is pleasant, because it is profitable, because it is socially acceptable. God wants us to love the truth. It is the water of life He offers us. Don't adulterate it with pollutants.

Love truth for its own sake, and it will come to you.

* * *

The one who claims to speak the oracles of God must expect to be asked many questions.

He can be asked, first of all, "Who are you to make this claim?"

Every "*I*" contains a multifaceted "we." We have within us a long history of *I's*, many sides of our personality. Which of my *I's* speaks oracles?

If the different faces of the self alternate and I think one thing at one time and something else at another, or if at times I live my unconscious life without thinking, then what happens in my mind at one moment can contradict what happened a few moments before, and I can be certain of nothing. Can something uncertain be the oracle of God?

To claim certainty is mostly a pose. It is not reasonable to always be certain, to know things absolutely, when every event has so many faces, most of which are beyond our ken anyway.

Furthermore, there is no such thing as a state of perpetual illumination. Just as it is impossible to be in a constant state of ecstasy or to stand on tiptoe without relaxation, so it is also impossible to administer truth 24 hours a day, although we may have access to it.

The apostle Peter said one day, under divine inspiration, that Jesus was the Son of God. After a few minutes, another "*I*" of Peter said such terrible things that Jesus called him "satan." Peter boasted that even if everyone else forsook Jesus, he would not. This was, again, another *I*; then he denied ever having known Jesus—another *I*. Later he repented with tears and received the commission to feed Jesus' sheep, which he also did. (See Matthew 16:17-23; Matthew 26:7; John 21:16-17.)

Legend says that when persecution erupted in Rome, Peter fled. Again, that was another *I*. While fleeing, he realized that what he was doing was wrong. He returned and died a martyr's death for Christ, asking to be crucified head-down because he did not deserve to die like Jesus. Peter had many *I's*. That is why he had three names in the Bible: Simon, Cephas, and Peter. It is this same Peter who teaches us in his epistle to speak the oracles of God. Which of the *I's* of Peter spoke oracles?

We all have many *I's*. I have had many opinions and convictions in life that I later abandoned. What then authorizes me to believe that today, as I write these lines, I am speaking the oracles of God? What about all the things I said yesterday? And what of that I will speak tomorrow?

How can one find out for himself which of his many opinions are the truth of God? Peter, the man who said so many wrong things and vacillated so much, who was publicly accused by St. Paul of pre-varication (Gal. 2:11ff), might have wondered him-self which of his sayings, if any, were oracles.

How can one choose among the many who claim to speak the oracles of God? Does an objective, sure truth exist? If so, how can one find it?

The oracle of God must tell me, first of all, what an oracle of God is and must then accredit itself as such. The question is an important one, a critical one, but don't try to get quick answers.

Foreign lecturers speaking in Japan have wondered why students don't reply to questions put to them. But in their culture an immediate reply shows contempt for the speaker. It means that his questions are of so little importance that anyone can answer them without difficulty. Therefore the proper reaction to a question is not a quick reply, but meditation upon it, indicating that the question and the questioner deserve respect.

The number of conflicts in families, churches, and society at large would be greatly reduced if spouses, children, parents, parties, leaders, and states would forego the felt need to respond immediately to every question and instead make each question an object of loving, or at least civil, mediation.

Therefore, my advice to you is not to swallow this book in a hurry. Read a portion, then meditate. To make this easier, I have divided the book into small, bite-size portions.

* * *

But is there no hurry to find the truth?

St. Augustine says, "You would never have sought the truth if you had not already found it." "The truth induces men to seek the truth," said St. Makarios the Great. And Blaise Pascal wrote, "We could not seek God unless in some real sense we already possessed Him." The fact that you seek truth, that you ask for it, shows you have a love for it. Love for truth is an essential part of truth itself. If you seek it earnestly, you can afford to sit down quietly, like Mary Magdalene.

Which is more real to you, your problem or yourself? You existed before you posed the question to yourself about finding truth. How many hours a day do you seek it even now? You are much bigger and more important than your search for truth.

Don't throw away the whole of your life for this particular, though valuable, preoccupation—this search for truth. Live your life. When you work, work. When you eat, eat. When you sleep, sleep. When you amuse yourself, amuse yourself. Truth and life are good companions. They are friends, not enemies. You don't have to exclude the one in order to have the other. Jesus said, "I am the Way." What does this "Way" consist of? He explained Himself immediately: "the Truth *and* the Life." (See John 14:6.)

Take it easy, take one step at a time, and you will reach the truth. Meanwhile, be yourself.

Truth is the supreme goal, except that truth alone can be found nowhere, just as one cannot find either iron or gold alone in the earth; they exist only in combination with other elements.

Jesus said, "I am the way, the truth *and* the life" (Jn. 14:6). If one wishes to know truth, he must know life too. If he wishes to fulfill the demands of truth, he must be attentive to the demands of life as well.

St. Paul taught us to beware of vain philosophy (Col. 2:8).

Long ago there lived a king who had a very valuable stallion. He appointed a watchman to do nothing else but guard the magnificent animal during the night. To satisfy his concerns, the king arose at night and went to the guard.

"What are you doing?" he asked.

"Well, your majesty, I was just reflecting on why a circle is round and a square rectangular."

The king exclaimed, "I am happy to have in my service a real philosopher. Just continue."

Later in the night, the king went again and asked the watchman, "What were you doing now?"

"I was trying to find out what happens to the hole in a bagel after it is eaten. I did not eat the hole, but notwithstanding it has disappeared."

The king was very pleased to have a soldier with such interesting thoughts. He came a third time and asked the watchman, "What now? What are you thinking?"

"Now I have a really serious problem. There was a stallion in the stable. It is no longer there. Where could it be?"

For the sake of philosophy, he had lost the stallion of truth.

Seek the truth, but be careful not to destroy your life and the lives of other men for the sake of philosophizing about truth. Without men, where will the truth settle and of what good will it be?

The story is told that Pol Pot, the Communist dictator of Cambodia, declared, "I have a truth that will make my people happy."

He was asked, "What if your people do not accept your formula of truth?"

He replied, "I will kill all those who oppose truth. Truth is for me above all things." Out of a population of five million, he killed two million of his own people.

This is the attitude of the inquisitors of all convictions. This is the philosophy of those who tyrannize their families, forcing them to accept what they consider as truth.

God says, "You shall therefore keep My statutes and My judgments, which if a man does, *he shall live by them...*" (Lev. 18:5).

Truth is given that you and others might live by it, not die by it.

Be careful. Be forewarned.

* * *

A sage had a disciple called Moses. When he called, the disciple would reply, "Yes," and come immediately. The master would then tell him a few things, but with a disappointed expression on his face. Moses did not understand why. Again and again, the master would call, "Moses!" Each time

Moses would reply, "Yes," and elicit the same reaction. Eventually he came to the conclusion that his answer "Yes" was not what his master desired.

He changed, and for a time, as often as the master called, "Moses!" he replied, "Here I am." But neither did this answer satisfy the sage, though he continued to impart love to his disciple and to teach him the ways of God.

One day Moses had an illumination, and when the master called, "Moses!" he came, smiled, and said, "I understood." With this, he left his master forever.

The master gave a sign of relief. Moses had become himself. He now knew he was Moses and no longer had to be the copy of his master.

Likewise, I urge you to develop a personality that is able to discern the truth among the many lies that are told.

* * *

You may be sure that truth exists. There is no doubt about this. Socrates already showed the fallacy of the contrary assertion.

The Sophist philosopher Gorgias had asserted, "Truth does not exist." Socrates challenged these words in a conversation with Kriton, a disciple of Gorgias. He asked the younger man, "Does Gorgias believe what he says?"

"Yes."

"Then Gorgias contradicts himself."

"How?"

"According to the teaching of your master, no truth exists, yet he considers this, his assertion, to be true. Then he does acknowledge something to be true."

No one can escape the belief that men can know a sure truth. If we say, "Everything we know is relative," then this knowledge of ours, that everything is known only relatively, is an absolute truth? Everything we postulate is based on just such an assumption. So there exists a kernel of the absolute even in the midst of relativity.

There exist sure oracles.

The Bible calls the Creator "The God of truth" (Ps. 31:5). There is a legend that the blood that flowed from Jesus on Golgotha formed the Hebrew words *Ani ha-emet*, "I am the truth." We can know a truth.

Socrates said, "I know that I know nothing." This assertion may exhibit modesty, but it can be accepted only with certain qualifications. It is simply not true that Socrates knew nothing. He knew the Greek language. He knew the whole alphabet. He knew grammar—substantives, verbs, conjugations. He knew how to think, how to speak. There always exists a core of sure truth at the heart of what is doubtful and relative in our thinking.

* * *

The problem is, we confuse knowing the truth with understanding it. "I have not understood a bar of music in my life, but I have felt it." said Igor Stravinsky. "I shut my eyes in order to see," said the painter Paul Gaugin.

Anna Pavlova, the renowned dancer, when asked once to explain her pirouettes, replied to the interviewer, "If I could say it, I would not have danced it." If painters could say, in words, what they know, they would not resort to the brush and the palette. Einstein and other creative scientists have expressed their need to think in images. Words alone cannot yield the truth.

I have learned much about God not only from the words of Christian hymns, but also from the Gregorian chanting in Orthodox churches and from the music of Bach and others.

Only a small part of truth can be understood: The rest must be caught as an intense longing for a beautiful, loving, harmonious world. Truth is something much better than a set of ideas.

* * *

All music critics evaluate the notes played on instruments. But what about the music of the pauses between the notes?

Before being confined in Communist prisons for fourteen years, I believed that the whole Bible as written was the truth. In jail I discovered that in reality I had considered as truth only the black letters of the Bible, without paying attention to the white spaces between the letters, words, and chapters.

In the Bible, Jesus is called "the Word," not the sentence. He is the Word surrounded by white space, the white margins and blank pages within the Bible. Many of the most interesting truths are written with invisible ink on these white spaces.

What did Jesus say to the priests when He conversed with them in the temple at the age of twelve? What did He do between twelve and thirty? What is meant by the assertion that after His crucifixion He descended into hell? What happened after the resurrection between the times He appeared to His disciples?

Learn also from the greater Christ of the white pages, and you will know.

* * *

All this may sound irrational, but what if some truth is irrational? It could not be otherwise because there is much that is beyond reason in the universe. Any effort to understand it only by rational means will be futile and superficial.

The chief features of the world are, at one pole, conflict and struggle, the clash of antithetical forces, and at the opposite pole, ardent love. Human life is not all rational. It is a madman like Hitler beguiling the German people, then considered rational, with the senseless slogan "Blood and soil," and a loving priest like Maximilian Kolbe throwing away his life in Auschwitz for a man he never knew. To tell an SS officer he wanted to die in place of another prisoner was foolish. Logic would have taught him that the officer would laugh and kill them both.

Bergson said in *Creative Evolution*: "The intellect is characterized by a natural inability to comprehend life. Instinct, on the contrary, is molded on the very form of life."

In the search for truth, do not rely on intellect alone. *Golgotha* means in Aramaic "place of the skull." When Jesus was taken there, He was crucified. If you wish Him to live, bring Him to the place of the heart!

Use instinct, intuition, feeling, faith, a high ideal, a noble dream that should become the truth. Do not be the lackey of truth, saying only what it orders, but be its master and make of reality what your heart dictates in its best moments.

A certain painter, when reproached that his portraits did not look like the subject, replied that it was not his business to exactly replicate how a person looked, but to challenge the person to become like the picture he painted.

This is exactly how God paints the faithful soul. She is called in Scripture "the fairest among women," "A lily among thorns," "without spot or wrinkle" (Song 5:9; 2:2; Eph. 5:27). Rationalists would say this is simply not true. The description does not show the Church as it is. It was never God's intention merely to describe how it is, but to tell us how it should be. This is the image God has of us, and He expects us to conform to it.

It is interesting to note that only in the English language does the word translated "to realize" have the double meaning "to understand, to be aware of," and also "to cause something to be." This is how truth is molded.

* * *

Truth, when communicated in words, is no longer pure truth. It passes through a censorship.

The Wycliffe Bible translators on the Solomon Islands were fined a pig and ten dollars in cash for having used the name "Momoli" in a story in a reading primer. It was simply a contrived name, but it happened to coincide with name of an ancestor who was worshiped.

The translators soon found out they must be cautious. The common word for "sea"—*asi*—also had to be avoided because in the past it was the name of an important man. Now it was forbidden.

Another taboo is pronouncing the names of in-laws. Once in a church there was a Scripture reading from the Book of First Peter. The person who read the text accordingly said, "The reading this morning is from the first of my father-in-law, chapter one."

On Misima Island, off Papua, New Guinea, a person who had an in-law with a name that sounded like the word for "big" had to stop singing hymns whenever he came to that word. It was taboo.

We smile about these backward people. But can we express freely in "civilized" nations all we know to be true? Don't we often have to use euphemisms?

It is taboo to speak to children about one of the most dramatic aspects of life, which they will understand only when they are already involved in it. But then it is too late to learn.

In Germany after the defeat of Hitler, the word "fatherland" could no longer be used. It was considered a dirty word.

In psychoanalysis, both the patient and the doctor try to construct out of isolated threads a story that makes sense. When the psychoanalyst and his patient converse, they intentionally invest happenings with a coherence that may not have existed in reality. The facts of life are shaped to give them meaning and purpose. Both use literary skill.

We all try to give sense to everything, instead of acknowledging that nonsense is also part of reality.

A religious person usually romanticizes the story of his conversion. In Jesus' parable of the prodigal son, the youth, reduced to utter misery, returns to his father (who symbolizes God) for the simple reason that at home he would have better food. If the prodigal son had told the story himself, he might have said that a longing of his heart after Heaven made him return to his father's house.

It takes only one black sheep to prove that all sheep are not white. If there were only one deformation of truth, it would be enough to assure us that not all stories and thoughts parading as truth are true. But falsehoods are multiplied without number.

Humanity by itself has no truth and cannot obtain it. Truth can only descend to us from a higher sphere.

* * *

There exists an unconscious wisdom called faith. The smallest notion of the unconscious soul is more important and true than the noblest production of our conscious thoughts. God loves to dwell in the darkness of the unconscious. There resides the truth for which the conscious has to fish.

The Sufite Mohammedan sect has a legend about Jesus, told in a beautiful book by Indris Shah.

According to this legend, Jesus once saw a group of sad people who, when asked about their grief, replied, "We fear we may go to hell." Then He saw another group who also looked very depressed and wept.

"What troubles you?" He asked.

"We heard there is a splendid paradise, and we tremble that we might miss it."

Then He met a third group, all worn out but with faces full of joy. "What makes you so radiant?" He queried.

"Here and there we have obtained some little bits of truth, and we have within us a spirit that promises us even more. We now see things more and more as they really are. With what little truth we have, we realize that nothing else matters to us."

Jesus said, "These are the people who attain. They will see the face of God."

* * *

Seekers after truth generally begin with the presumption that truth is a response to the question "What?" This is wrong.

Pilate put the question, to which he got no reply: "What is truth?" (Jn. 18:38). Before him stood the incarnate Truth, but he did not recognize Him.

Pilate's question is like asking, "What is the melody of a peach?" He makes the false assumption that truth is the fruit of discussion, that it is a collection of statements.

The right question is, "*Who* is the truth?" Truth is a Person. Jesus said, "I am the truth" (Jn. 14:6). Jews search the Scriptures; Buddhists search their canons; Muslims search the Koran. Jesus says, "The Scriptures testify of Me. Come to Me" (Jn. 5:39; Mt. 11:28). Since He promises to live within us, in the measure to which we become like Him, we too can become the truth.

There are no right answers to wrong questions.

In many places in the New Testament, "Jesus" is not just the name of one Person. He is called *ho Iesous*—"the Jesus." He bears a generic name. There exists a category of men to whom the name Jesus can be applied at least partially. These are truth-bearers. They represent Jesus. In Kabbalistic poetry they are called "the minuscule faces of God."

St. Laurence Justinian wrote, "He thirsted for us and desired to give Himself to us." Well, He has done so, which means the truth is in us.

We might not realize it most of the time because of not differentiating between what theologians call *fides directa* and *fides reflecta*—direct and reflected faith. If I say "I believe," I say what I believe to believe I can believe I am a believer and be mistaken. Some, on the other hand, have a direct faith and are not aware of it or are aware only rarely.

But if Jesus lives within us, we are the people to whom John writes: "But you have an anointing of the Holy One, and you *know* all things. I have not written to you because you do not know the truth, but because you know it" (1 Jn. 2:20,21).

Buddha's last words were, "Seek the truth." Jesus said, "I am the truth." Therefore His disciples are no more searchers for truth but its possessors.

Scripture says that God "...raised us up together, and made us sit together in the heavenly places in Christ Jesus" (Eph. 2:6). Observe, "we are raised up" and "sit in heavenly places."

Scientists have launched a space telescope that is clear-sighted because of its position above the atmosphere, which bends, distorts and absorbs light before it reaches the earth. The night sky cannot properly be seen from the earth, any more than objects can be viewed through a fish tank filled with water. Light passing through the atmosphere, or water, is refracted and therefore dislocates the objects being viewed. Furthermore, air and water turbulence blur the images. A space telescope remedies all these defects.

If we look at truth from the earth, we are unable to see it as and where it is, but with Jesus we are seated high above the world in heavenly places where God's peace reigns undisturbed and undistorted. There we become possessors of the truth as it really is.

Chapter 2

Love the Truth

In the search for truth, we are doomed to meet innumerable speculators, eccentrics, crackpots, and out-and-out fakers, not to mention their gullible victims. Even St. Paul recognized that some of those who taught were largely unreliable. He warned against the "many vain talkers and deceivers" in the early church (Tit. 1:10).

Psychologist Bertram Forer bought a newsstand astrology book, from which he extracted the following character reading: "...You are extroverted, affable, sociable, while at other times you are introverted, wary and reserved. Disciplined and controlled on the outside, you tend to be worrisome and insecure on the inside. Your sexual adjustment has presented some problems for you..."

This very same character reading was given to fifty students, who were each made to believe it was uniquely formulated for him as a result of a personality test. Forty-one percent of the students considered it a perfect fit to their personality.

Most of us tend to be gullible and are easily waylaid by countless individuals and organizations eager to lead us astray. A psychologist, Hyman, convinced that he could read palms, decided one day to tell people the exact opposite of what he read in their palms. He found that they swallowed what he said as readily as before.

In a Seattle bus station a woman went to the restroom, leaving her bags by her seat. Profiting from her absence, a man rummaged through her baggage and disappeared with something bundled under his coat. When the woman returned, she cried, "My tape deck was stolen!" Several men who witnessed the incident agreed to give their names and addresses for use in the insurance claim. When they were questioned later, they recalled the color, shape, and size of the tape deck.

The fact is that there never had been a tape deck. The whole incident was staged as an experiment by the University of Washington to show the unreliability of witnesses and of human memory.

* * *

If we wish to have the truth, we must realize we have nothing to rely on. Truth can come only as a free gift from above. It is received as revelation or not at all.

The Romans had a saying: *Quidquid recipitur, secundum modum recipientis recipitur*—"Whatever is received, is received according to the manner of the one receiving it." Aristotle said, "Wickedness corrupts a man's nature and gives him false principles and evil measures of things." Bad men are condemned to have false ideas. And we are all bad.

Jesus, the Pure, cleanses us from all sins. He, the embodiment of truth, identifies with us and becomes our new personality. He gives us His thoughts.

Those with ears only for what is earthly believe that music consists of the sounds produced by crickets rubbing their legs together. But those who look up will hear the heavenly harmony of truth.

Just as pigeons or snails have a magnetic sense that helps orient them at great distances, so those who hear the sound of ultimate truth are irresistibly attracted to it. They know to whom they are to entrust themselves and where they are going. Jesus told us, "Where I go you know, and the way you know" (Jn. 14:4).

Lady Philosophy will criticize us immediately, saying, "Wait a bit. You jumped from the search for truth to the unwarranted assertion that Jesus is the truth. Why Jesus?"

Are we obliged to justify ourselves before her? What are her credentials? And who is she? From whence is her right to interrogate and investigate?

And who are the philosophers? How much do they love me? Who among them sacrificed a heaven for me? Who among them died on a cross for me?

If religion enters into a discussion with philosophy, its doom is unavoidable. Debating philosophy is a good way to commit spiritual suicide. A Romeo would not think of trying to justify before philosophy his sentiments for Juliet. Nor will we define ourselves before the philosophic sowers of doubt.

The oracle says that Jesus is the truth. Where the oracle has spoken, let all else keep silent.

Ultimate truth is not something to be analyzed or debated. It is something to be practiced.

That Jesus is the truth is an essential fact of human life that only ignorance can deny.

* * *

The truth has come.

Maritain wrote, "Henceforth, God remains dumb, and has nothing to say, because what He said in times past to the prophets in a fragmentary manner has now been totally said. He gave us His all, which is His son, which means that to try now to interrogate God or to will to have a vision or a revelation does not only mean stupidity, it is also an offense toward God. We should have our eyes fixed on Christ without seeking anything else.

"God could tell you, 'If I have revealed all things to you in my Word, which is my Son, I have no other

Word with which to reply or reveal more than that. Fix your eyes upon Him because in Him I have told you everything. I reveal everything to you, and you will find in Him more than what you desire or ask....

" 'You desire words and fragments of revelations; but if you fix your eyes upon Him, you will find everything because He is my entire world, and my entire answer. He is my whole vision and revelation. You have all the answers. I have given you the reply—as brother, teacher and companion, atonement, and reward.' "

It seems Maritain was very sure that God had said everything through Christ. Just one little thing was lacking—that Maritain would add his assurance of Christ's relaxation. My oracle might also be needed as well as the private revelations that some children of God received.

* * *

"Joseph, son of David, do not be afraid to take to you Mary...." So said the angel (Mt. 1:20b).

I was also afraid to take Mary into my life and into my love. Then I heard the same words spoken to Joseph. Now she is part of my life too, as well as Joseph and the multitude of angels who prepared for and were present at Jesus' birth.

Mary was obedient when the archangel Gabriel told her God desired that she give birth to the Messiah. She was a faithful Jewess who may have known the prophecies. She may have known from

Isaiah 53 that her child would be "a man of sorrows acquainted with grief." She may have also known from Psalm 22 that "they [would] pierce His hands and His feet" on a cross, that He would be rejected by His people, an object of scorn, that His whole life would be full of pain.

She may have known that the calling to be the mother of God's Son was a call to suffer with her child for 33 years and in the end to stand weeping at the foot of the cross. Her quiet acceptance was heroic: "Let it be to me according to your word" (Lk. 1:38).

Joseph's decision was also remarkable. He had loved a pure girl and was sure they would have a blessed marriage and would have children to rear in the fear of the Lord. Then his heart was stricken at the discovery that his bride was pregnant. Whose heart would not have been? She never gave him any explanation. Then an angel told him in a dream that what she had conceived was of the Holy Spirit.

Joseph probably knew little about what or who the Holy Spirit was. Such a thing had never happened before. Such a message was not easy to believe. But he must have been a man who always put the best construction on events, even if it didn't seem advisable given difficult circumstances. He decided to obey the dream.

The experience had been hard on both bridegroom and bride. Mary became taciturn and "pondered these things in her heart." Only a few of her words are reported for 33 years of her life with Jesus. As for Joseph, we are not told of a single word he ever spoke.

The two spent their lives quietly in simple belief. When you have Jesus for a child, there is no need for much talk.

We too have to receive Jesus in faith, even while realizing that we must bear a cross and be crucified with Him.

What proof did Joseph have that the dream was not just a dream? The search for proof comes from doubt, and disbelief is sinful. Atheists may find it difficult to believe, but believers find it difficult to entertain doubt. Disbelief to them is as abhorrent as adultery or killing.

Only those who do not know Jesus question the logical legitimacy of faith. Mary did not doubt when an angel spoke. Neither did Joseph, even if the angel appeared to him only in a dream. How then should we doubt the One who died for us?

When we came to believe in Jesus, it was not the result of reasoning on our part that could very well have been false. When Peter first acknowledged Jesus as the Son of the living God, the Lord assured him, "...flesh and blood has not revealed this to you, but My Father who is in heaven" (Mt. 16:17). This also applies to my faith.

We throw in our lot with Jesus because He has the seeds of truth that contain the fruits of righteousness and the flowers of eternity. What philosophers and doubters have to offer is, by comparison, mere husks.

* * *

Jesus is repeatedly referred to as the Mediator. A mediator never represents only one side—he hears the grievances of both parties and seeks a middle way of peace.

God has many grievances against men. They sin against His law, although as Creator He has the right to require obedience.

In Isaiah 5:1-3 there is a song that is God's complaint:

Now let me sing to my Well-beloved
A song of my Beloved regarding His vineyard:
My Well-beloved has a vineyard
On a very fruitful hill.
He dug it up and cleared out its stones,
And planted it with the choicest vine.
He built a tower in its midst.
And also made a winepress in it;
So He expected it to bring forth
good grapes,
But it brought forth wild grapes.
And now, O inhabitants of Jerusalem
and men of Judah,
Judge, please, between Me and My vineyard.

Then God asks the question, "What more could have been done to my vineyard?" (Is. 5:4)

Isaiah had no answer to this question. God did. He knew mankind's complaints were justified, too. And He did the one thing more that could be done: He came to share human life with all its hardships. How can one reproach a God who is a poor, suffering man just like you? A God who permits pain must show He is ready to bear it Himself. This is what Jesus did when He became God in the flesh. He also satisfied the just demands of God to the human soul. He paid the ransom for us. He bore the punishment for our sins. This is how peace was established.

A pastor stayed overnight at a farm. In the morning the farmer showed him his chicken house. They paused before a nest on which a hen was seated. Under her wings she sheltered her chicks. "Touch her, pastor," said the farmer. She was cold, dead, unmoving. A weasel had sucked out all her blood, but to protect the chicks, which the weasel would also have attacked, she had not moved.

Such a mediator we have in Jesus.

We may have grievances against God. Jesus did not take His defense in many words, though He said, "No one is good but God." Neither did He quarrel with sinners, but simply showed them His love and then died for them.

On Good Friday He was dead, but under His wings lay the assurance of life. Only a week before, He had lamented over His people, "How often I wanted to gather your children together, as a hen gathers her chicks under her wings, and you were not willing!" (Mt. 23:37b).

Because Jesus is just such a mediator, He split time in two. Recorded history divides time into the era before Christ and the rest after Christ (*Anno Domini*—in the year of our Lord). Even those who hate Him number the years from His birth.

* * *

During the French Revolution in 1789, a certain Lepaux launched a new religion called "Theophilanthropy." It made no headway, though supported by the government.

Lepaux complained to Talleyrand, a witty statesman, and asked for advice. Talleyrand replied. "There is a sure way to make your religion popular. Get yourself crucified, buried, and then resurrected on the third day. It would be advisable also to perform some miracles, to heal a multitude of the sick, to feed the hungry, and to bring a couple of dead men back to life."

This is how Jesus introduced His religion. This is how He became our Master—master in the absolute sense of the word. When He was still a babe, Simeon called Him "Lord," using for it the Greek word that means "despot" (Lk. 2:29). He is an absolute monarch with unlimited power who is obligated to give account to no one for what He does. Therefore just to question His authority is sin.

Though endowed with all power, He does not exercise it. He does not dictate. Rather, He reduced Himself to our level and became a man like us, in fact, a man of low social rank. And He "was in all points tempted as we are" (Heb. 4:15). Therefore this almighty "despot" can be our understanding friend.

Father Brown, the central character in Chesterton's crime novels, could easily detect murderers and robbers, because he could feel what was happening in someone else's soul. He knew the potential thief, crook and assassin within himself; he was attentive to the bad impulses of his own heart. He knew what he would do it were he to follow these evil inclinations. By identifying with lawbreakers, by infiltrating their skewed mentality, he was able to follow leads invisible to others.

Jesus, by identifying with mankind, was subject to like temptations—which must have caused Him untold suffering beyond anything we know because He never yielded to them. His encounters with evil enabled Him to have great understanding even for the worst of sinners, even for His betrayer and murderers. He identified completely with them. Their sins became His, and He bore their punishment. The "despot" with complete, absolute power consented to die a malefactor's death on a cross.

Therefore God greatly exalted Him (see Phil. 2:9).

Bethlehem is a town connected with the name of two despots. Jesus was born there. Herod was buried there. Herod, who severely exercised his despotic powers, is dead, and who knows what lies beyond? Jesus, who renounced His despotic powers, still lives and will dwell with His beloved forevermore.

Every one of us has the potential to dominate someone else. Let us learn how to use this potential from the example of Jesus.

* * *

St. John Berchman wrote these beautiful passages in the seventeenth century:

"Think of Jesus Christ raised up on the cross praying for His enemies; see how His blood flows from every wound...Looking at the head of our Lord crowned with thorns, I will pray for my superiors, both ecclesiastical and civil. Considering the wound in His right hand, I will pray for my relatives, for my brothers, my friends and benefactors. The wound in the left hand will remind me to pray for my enemies, for those who have offended me, for all those whom I myself have caused to be saddened.

"For myself, I will take the wound in His sacred side; I will ask Him for these graces:

"1. to love God with all my heart;

"2. to be on fire with zeal for the salvation of my fellow men;

"3. to persevere in my vocation...

"Seeing the feet of Jesus pierced with nails, I will remember to pray for all, both good and bad."

The images of even the most renowned men of all time pale into insignificance when viewed in the light of Jesus, the Son of righteousness.

An anonymous poet compared Jesus with Alexander the Great, the Macedonian emperor who conquered all the countries from Greece to Egypt in the third century B.C.:

"Jesus and Alexander died at thirty-three;
one lived and died for self,
one died for you and me.
One died upon a throne,
the other on a cross;
one's life a triumph seemed,
the other's but a loss.

"One led vast armies forth,
the other walked alone;
one shed a whole world's blood,
the other gave His own.
One won the world in life,
and lost it all in death;
the other lost His life,
to win the whole world's faith.

"Jesus and Alexander died at thirty-three;
one died in Babylon,
and one in Calvary.

One gained all for himself,
and one Himself He gave.
One conquered every throne,
the other every grave."

In Shakespeare's *King Lear*, the good is defeated. Cordelia, the king's only faithful daughter, lies dead at the feet of her father who had unjustly rejected her. In all great dramas—as in real life—everything ends in death. Oedipus, Medea, and Clytemnestra; and Macbeth, Othello, and all the Richards and Henrys of Shakespeare's plays—all conclude with the great personalities dead and the curtain falling. What they accomplished, good or bad, was for nought.

John Berchman made the wounds of Jesus his subject of meditation. I also meditate on them. But where are these wounds? They are in the glorified body of Jesus, in the body with which He triumphed over death. He showed them to Thomas, and all the apostles saw them as proof of the resurrection.

He assured us, too, of a glorious resurrection.

Worms, fire, or the sea might consume my body. But my spirit will live in a world with no more wanderings and trials. I do not have to pass through many painful incarnations. Beyond death lies paradise.

Chapter 3

The Measure of the Soul

The medieval mystic Eckhart wrote, "If you ask how big the soul is, you should know that heaven and earth cannot comprehend its grandness, but only God alone, who cannot be comprehended by all the heavens."

Long before Eckhart's time, Heraclitus (2500 B.C.) had said, "If you wish to arrive at the limits of your soul, you will not find them no matter which way you go, so great are its depths."

Even if you do not believe the soul to be immortal, you must acknowledge that it has been considered as such by the greatest spirits of mankind, that the soul would deserve to be transmitted to a permanent sphere, and that it would be good if it could bloom in another world and still be useful.

The Greek philosopher Plato wrote,

"The man whose heart is directed toward love of teaching and wisdom and who exercises this part in himself, will surely have immortal and divine thoughts if he apprehended truth. And in the measure in which it is in human nature to have immortality, he will not miss it."

How little do men value their own soul! Eve sold hers for an apple, Esau for a plate of lentils, and Judas for thirty pieces of silver.

Be careful that you do not sell yours.

* * *

The Greek philosopher Plotinus wrote,

"Often when I fall asleep and leave the external world, I come to myself. Then I see a wonderful beauty. I believe strongly in my belonging to a better and higher world. I live within myself...the most splendid life...[in union]...with Godhead. After having sojourned with the Godhead, when I descend to the activity of the body, I ask myself why I am descending and how come my soul ever entered a body when it was what it had revealed itself to me to be, in spite of its inhabiting a body."

Plotinus had experienced a portion of his soul through a dream. It is true that no one has ever seen his world, but neither have we seen our pain or our joy. We simply feel them.

It is nonsense to seek the seat of the soul, because, like life itself, it can be "everywhere."

For years I lived alone in a subterranean Communist prison cell. In solitary confinement we had no books, no radio. There was no voice, no whisper. Perfect silence reigned. No one ever spoke to us.

But in those years I mentally visited relatives and friends, those alive and those who had died. I remembered many churches in many lands; I thought of other spheres, of angels and glorified saints in Heaven, of devils in hell, of Adam and Eve, and of the generation that will witness Jesus' return.

The soul only visits this material world, but since we do not belong to it, the soul cannot find here the explanation for or definition of itself. It is so different from all that is in this world that it sometimes doubts if it is at all, in the sense this world gives to the word "is." Jesus says of His disciples, "Theirs is the kingdom of heaven" (Mt. 5:3)—now, not in the future.

The soul is the Kingdom's most exquisite toy.

Jesus says, "The kingdom of God is within you" (Lk. 17:21), but not all of it is illuminated. The last words of Goethe, the great German poet, were, "Light, more light!"

This we should all seek. May this book aid you in the search.

* * *

Scientists have sought the locus of the soul in laboratories and during autopsies. They have never found it, nor will they ever. It belongs outside the realm of the objects of the inquest.

What then is the soul, and where is it?

It may be that we are trying to solve a problem that is essentially meaningless. The noted British physicist Sir James Jeans wrote, "It is probably as meaningless to discuss how much room an electron takes up as it is to discuss how much room fear and anxiety or an uncertainty takes up." Matter might not be material at all. Perhaps the soul is not a "something" to be found "somewhere."

Lightning strikes. An artist can paint the splendid flash of light in the dark sky. A scientist describes it as a electrical discharge in the atmosphere. For Luther, lightning was the sign of God's wrath that propelled him into becoming a monk. Which of these perceptions is correct?

A mental event is described by the neurologist as an interplay of nerves, brain cells, and hormones. Shakespeare's Romeo and the early Christians did not even know that hormones existed, yet Romeo died for Juliet, and early believers gave their lives for the ecstasy of their faith.

Will, sentiment, and thought are connected with the body and can be explained in terms of the body. But the contrary is also true. The body and its functions are mental concepts. Our mind tells us (who is the "us" and who does the telling, and who analyzes the relationship between teller and told?) that the different senses give it a multitude of perceptions which it synthesizes into the notion of a "body."

Without a body there is no mind. Without a mind, is there no body, but simply a whirlwind of elementary particles? These too are a product of the mind.

Poets and painters tell us about sunsets. Scientists enjoy the portrayal but are also convinced the sun neither rises nor sets; the earth turns around the sun. Which is the truth? Why should science be the truth, and art and everyday experience not be?

When I speak objectively, I limit myself to physiology and anatomy. Thinking as subject, I know my soul.

Virtually everyone lives in the presumption that space is a kind of receptacle within which things are located. A handful of scientifically trained people know that space is an attribute of matter. It is a relationship between things and would not exist without things.

The scientists who think thus also live and walk around in space and create spaceships.

Souls exist just as all the beauties of nature exist, no matter how much scientists might want to reduce them to cold chemical or physical formulas.

This soul can live eternally in happiness and usefulness, or it can get lost through persistence in sin, refusal of repentance, and denial of faith.

If you proposed to an ass, "I will give you enough straw to fill a house if you will allow me to cut off your head," the ass would not accept. But we accept such proposals as often as we sin.

We are like a man who has a costly jewel in the safe but cares more about the safe than the jewel. Observing how well Westerners treat their pets, one might prefer to be their pet than their soul.

Jesus has come to save your soul. Listen to Him!

* * *

An equilibrist stands upside down on a broomstick teetering over several shaky tables and plays the violin. A person in the audience leans over and says to his friend, "I wonder why he plays the violin in public. He's not a virtuoso."

This is how many people adjudge the thoughts of Christian prisoners wrenched from them in extremes of physical and psychological torture.

I shared and viewed the sufferings of many fellow prisoners in an underground Communist prison. What intrigued us most was that we did not obtain from Heaven what it was obviously reasonable to expect: a slight improvement in our situation, food to quiet our hunger, an abatement of the cruel torture. We did not get what we expected because Heaven is not—humanly speaking—reasonable.

Jesus said, "There will be more joy in heaven over one sinner who repents than over ninety-nine just persons who need no repentance" (see Lk. 15:7). This is surely not reasonable.

Jesus also said, "To whom little is forgiven, the same loves little" (Lk. 7:47b). Why should one first have to commit many heinous sins before loving Him? Therese of Lisieux objected to these words. Brought up in a devout family, dedicated to the Lord at a very early age, a Carmelite nun at 15, dead at 24, she used to say to the Lord, "I love you much, ardently, though I had not known the great sins of the world."

Nowhere does the Bible speak about the reasonableness of God, but rather about His foolishness (1 Cor. 1:21). He is as unreasonable as the thoughts of little children. Christ became a child and recommended that we become as children too.

The renowned Franciscan Giacopone was considered mad because of the things he did out of love for Jesus. It is said that once even Jesus appeared to him and asked, "Why do you commit such mad deeds?" He replied, "Because You taught me. If I am mad, You are even more so. Where is the reasonableness of Your dying for me? I am a fool because Thou hast been a greater fool."

A newspaper published the story of a man whose hat was blown off while he was out fishing with friends. Quickly he jumped into the icy water to retrieve it and was never seen again. What a tragedy to risk a life for a hat worth a few dollars!

Was it reasonable to sacrifice the life of the unique Son of God for witless, dirty, dumb sheep? I have asked many shepherds what they would do if they saw a wolf. They all replied, "We would run for our lives." No man dies for sheep. Yet Jesus did. He died for beings worse than sheep—for those who denied and betrayed Him, for those who demanded His crucifixion. He died for His killers, for all who blaspheme and hate God.

Do not be surprised if you fail to get from God what you might reasonably expect. If He were truly reasonable, He would never listen to the prayers of people like us, nor would we have salvation.

Rather, God loves to the point of folly.

If you are in the sad situation of experiencing neither His reason nor His mad love, you might consider the fact that in the parable of the ninety and nine, only the lost sheep had sure proof of His love and concern. The others could reasonably say they were neglected and abandoned. When the prodigal son returned home, he was embraced with love, given a ring, and feted with the fatted calf, music, and dancing. The faithful son who came in from the fields all tired out and sweaty was not even greeted with a kind word.

Those who are faithful should simply be glad that others experience His love to folly.

The good Samaritan of the parable was not a tourist. He doubtless was making an important business trip and had appointments to keep. His extraordinary good deed must have delayed him considerably. Perhaps he even neglected other duties because he stopped to serve a wounded man.

While in solitary confinement, I waited for years for God to come to my aid. I realized that He tarried and tried to think of Him as the good Samaritan. I was sure He had set out to help but that He Himself might have seen a wounded man whom He stopped to succor and carry to the inn. I thought that He who saw a sparrow fall might also stop to brush the dew from a flower petal weighted down. In solitary, we were happy about His mad love even in moments when we were not its recipients.

Enraptured, Mary Magdalene of Pazzi ran about her convent carrying an image of the crucified Jesus and crying, "O Love, Love! I shall never cease, my God, to call you 'Love.' " She told the sisters, "He too is mad with love."

Do not count on reasonableness in Heaven and you will never be disappointed. Count only on the fact that there is One who loves you to such folly that He died for you. In response, forget about sweet reason and let yourself fall madly in love with Him. These, my words, are oracles of God.

* * *

To learn from your enemies is the best way to love them because it makes you thankful for them.

Jesus' command that we love our enemies is very different from what the world prescribes. Frederick the Great, king of Prussia, once said, "He is a fool, and that nation is a fool, that, having the power to strike his enemy unawares, does not strike and strike him the deadliest."

To the contrary, in Judaism, love for others is considered a duty.

In *Baba Quama*, a part of the Talmud, there is an example of some of the beautiful attitudes of love taught by the Jews: "If a companion calls you an ass and asks you to carry him like an ass, put the saddle on yourself immediately." It is better to suffer more injury than to lose your temper. It is better to be among the afflicted than those who afflict.

A very old Amish bishop taught me, "If someone shouts at you or wrongs you, put a thermometer in your mouth immediately to be sure your temperature does not rise."

If someone becomes your adversary, remember that many men are better than they look. There are evil spirits trying to control and direct their lives. Who knows from what pits of corruption they may have arisen? They might not have had opportunity to see the world from an angelic viewpoint.

The Sufites have a beautiful saying: "He who is not my friend, may God be his friend; and he who bears ill will against me, may his joy increase. He who puts thorns in my way on account of enmity, may every flower that blossoms in the garden of his life be without thorns."

In Gethsemane, Jesus called Judas (his betrayer) "Friend."

Chapter 4

Discern Between Truth and Illusion

There is certain truth: Where lies the difficulty in finding it?

In a free country, many real events take place about which a man can be informed through the media. If he desires, he can check his information by telephoning, writing, or even by traveling to the place where the events took place.

For many years I was a prisoner in a solitary cell without the slightest means of communication with the outside world. There was the world of reality, but I was in no position to ascertain the truth about it because I was in jail.

There is such a thing as truth, but we all are prisoners—of time, space, and our own surroundings. Supposing that ultimate truth lies outside of time and space, what possibility do I have of finding it?

A man in a bar asked the bartender, "Billy, do you know what time it is?"

"Two o'clock in the morning," was the reply.

The drunkard commented thickly, "I'm probably crazy. I've been drinking since yesterday morning and have been asking people again and again what time it is, and everyone has a different answer."

We are all caught in time. Because time flows, it enters into conflict with our convictions, which tend to be fixed. "I know what I believe. Don't confuse me with the facts," we say, half-joking. But time constantly brings new facts.

Every time you meet a man, you meet someone different from the one you knew before or who has been described to you. But too often, after one or more meetings with a person, we form an opinion that we tend to cling to, whether good or bad. This opinion, which is progressively more difficult to change, epitomizes our view of natural, psychological, and social reality.

Because we humans are prisoners of space, for thousands of years we accepted as truth the notion that the sun travels around the earth. Now we have discovered that this is an optical illusion. But what if our current belief is only another optical illusion that will be uncovered in future centuries?

A man with defective eyesight may imagine that he sees flies on his plate, for him they have full reality. Though the flies are not real, the illusion is.

The experience of our phenomenal world is like that of the short-sighted man. We all labor under the constant illusion of perceiving things where, in fact, there is only emptiness.

In Brahman initiations, after a very old ritual, when the disciple asks what the world is, the priest swings around a firebrand, which then resembles a solid wheel of flame. This visual response was a splendid foresight of modern science. We now know that, contrary to ancient beliefs, there exists no solid world. We ourselves consist of and are surrounded by a whirlwind of elementary particles which, because of the rapidity of their movement and the limitations of our senses, appear to be solid bodies.

Circling at crazy speeds, the particles can look like a bowl into which one can place "solid" objects. The nonexistent "bowl" can hold the nonexistent "objects." What exists is only the circling of ultramicroscopic particles.

The world is like a firebrand swung around in a circle. It took us thousands of years to come to this knowledge, but we do not know if this will be considered the "real thing" after yet another thousand years, if our imprisonment in time and space does not keep us from going even further in our discoveries.

For many prisoners in solitary confinement, the walls of the cell are the ultimate limits of their reality. Free men also have limits—of time, space, and surroundings.

One thing further: our only means of knowing the truth, our only instrument for apprehending it, seems to be the mind. But to the works of the mind one can apply the same things that Isaiah, the Jewish prophet, wrote some 3,000 years ago about idolatry:

The craftsman stretches out his rule, he marks it out with chalk; he fashions it with a plane, and he marks it out with a compass, and makes it like the figure of a man, according to the beauty of a man; that it may remain in the house. He cuts down cedars for himself, and takes the cypress and the oak; he secures it for himself among the trees of the forest. He plants a pine, and the rain nourishes it. Then it shall be for a man to burn, for he will take some of it and warm himself; yes, he kindles it and bakes bread; indeed he makes a god and worships it; he makes it a carved image, and falls down to it. He burns half of it in the fire; with this half he eats meat; he roasts a roast, and is satisfied. He even warms himself and says, "Ah! I am warm, I have seen the fire" and the rest of it he makes into a god, his carved image. He falls down before it and worships it, prays to it, and says, "Deliver me, for thou art my god!" (Isaiah 44:13-17)

Are not the worshipers of the mind guilty of the same thing? With a part of the mind we think about how to make a living; with another part we seek fun or amusement; with a part we compose jokes or poetry; with a part we sometimes dream foolish things; and then with another part of this same mind we conceive a god and bow before it—or what is worse, we deny the very existence of God and the need for Him.

We search for truth with the same mind that composes jokes and fantasizes in dream; that seeks high status in society and picks up a girl in a bar; that creates a beautiful poem and drowns its sensibilities in alcohol or drugs. Then we believe in the product of such an unfastidious mind.

In the Romanian language, the word for "mind" literally means "it lies," because the mind, by its very structure, can only tell lies.

What does the mind know? Its work is done by the brain. What does the mind know about its own brain?

The "text" of the genes of a single *e. coli* bacterium cell consists of four million symbols. The human brain is a network of some ten billion nerve cells, each of which has 200,000 contacts with neighboring cells. This huge mechanism, in addition to controlling all sorts of bodily functions, creates symphonies and dirty jokes, decides how to fight for an ideology or religion or rob a bank, plans to woo or deceive, thinks to speak or keep silence. And some of what it thinks, it declares to be the truth. Again, how reliable is this complex organism?

We see stars in the sky that we know disappeared a long time ago. We see them as fixed, though they move. We have corrected and intensified our eyesight by the use of telescopes. But what if the telescope only magnifies an illusion that will be discovered years hence—supposing, of course, that mankind survives his succession of illusions?

The Bible says of a previous age, "Every intent of the thoughts of [man's] heart was only evil continually" (Gen. 6:5b).

In such a context, truth seems unattainable. Therefore the psalmist prayed, "Lead me to the rock that is higher than I" (Ps. 61:2). The rock that a child finds impossible to climb is within reach if his father lifts him up. This is what God does for us.

* * *

If you can't find the truth, stand without it and love.

St. John of the Cross said, "On the evening of life, we will be judged according to love." Augustine wrote, "Lord, send into my heart sentiments of clemency so that, being drawn by love of truth, I will never lose the truth of love." St. Francis de Sales echoed these sentiments: "Truth which is not charitable ceases to be the truth, because in God, who is the supreme source of truth, charity is inseparable from truth."

Love must embrace the wicked as well as the good. It is said of St. Paissy that when he prayed for one of his disciples who had abandoned Christ, the Lord told him, "Paissy, are you praying for the one who has denied me?" Undisturbed, Paissy continued to pray for this man. "Paissy," the Lord then said to him, "you have equaled me in love."

This is how God enables true Christians to think and act.

It is related that when St. John the evangelist was extremely old, his disciples were wearied of his constant repetition of the words, "Little children, love one another." It seemed that this was all he said. When he was carried into their assembly, they asked him why he always repeated these words. "Because," he replied, "it is the Lord's commandment, and if only this one were fulfilled, it would be enough."

Not fulfilling this commandment is the greatest hindrance to the conversion of peoples and nations. No miracle can suffice where there is no love. It is all-powerful and all-inclusive. It centers in God, and God *is* love.

* * *

Jesus taught and demonstrated that we should love our enemies. In doing so, we may learn that people often have many faces.

A person's angry words may not actually be directed at their recipient. The anger may have other motivations.

Frustrated people who cannot convince others of their merits often stir up a great deal of hostility against themselves. Then they feel consoled by believing that these "enemies" stand in the way of the acknowledgment their merits deserve.

If we are having difficulty with "enemies," it would be profitable to ask ourselves if we are engendering this hostility. Are we are behaving like those who irritate us? Are our convictions about them indeed well-founded? Are there overtures we can make to break the bonds of ill will? The history of mankind would have been vastly different if individuals in both high and low positions would have stopped to examine their own hearts and motivations.

Therefore, it is better to love than to hate your enemy because you may not be properly informed about his state of mind. Perhaps you are both seeking truth. Be careful to defend your cause without harming the one who attacks you.

* * *

Don't ask many people about the truth. Rather keep silent. "…The Lord is in His holy temple. Let all the earth keep silence before Him" (Hab. 2:20).

I greatly miss silence in churches. For years I lived in perfect silence in my solitary underground cell in Communist prisons and have embraced it as a friend.

There have been countless studies about the words of the Bible, but none about its silence on a multitude of subjects that are worthy of notice.

Most of the great problems of life that concern us certainly troubled such men as Moses and the apostles, all of who met God face to face. Surely they asked difficult questions and received some answers about which the Bible is silent.

A sage once sat in profound meditation. He was asked, "Where is God?" The sage kept silent. The man repeated his question. Again, silence. The question was put the third time. Still, no reply.

"Don't you want to answer?" the man asked.

Finally, the sage said, "I replied, but you did not hear. God dwells in silence."

The Bible not only reveals many things, but it also keeps silence about many things. What did Jesus think and do between the ages of twelve and thirty? We find no answer to this in the Bible, not because there is a secret to be hidden but because such answers are communicated in silence.

Jesus was a marvelous preacher, but He also knew how to keep silence. He was silent before Herod, thus teaching him that soon his foul mouth would be silenced by death. He was silent when Pilate asked Him, "Where are You from?" (Jn. 19:9). Pilate should have understood that He was from the realm of silence.

The historian Macrobius relates that in Crete and Egypt, when worshipers came to the temple, they found it locked. A priest called "the keeper of the threshold" stood at the door and asked, "Do you know what house you are entering?" They were obliged to reply, "We know." They were then asked, "Do you know before whom you will stand?" They answered, "We know." Only then was the door unlocked. The worshipers thus had time to compose themselves before appearing in the presence of God.

The Spirit of adoption makes us cry out "Abba! Father!" (Rom. 8:15). Not much more is needed. A little child embraces his father's leg and simply says lovingly, "Daddy!" Moved by the spontaneous expression of love, the father will surely do his utmost for the child, for he knows better than the child what is best.

Let us speak to God and for God, but—most importantly—let us also have our times of deep silence.

Surely we must pray in words, but let us not neglect silent prayer. Francis de Sales says that in this "the soul becomes quiet wax, waiting for God to impress on it His word."

As long as one prays in words, there are two: God and the soul. In sacred silence, the two become one. The ability to remain silent in God's arms is the measure of love for God. Mary Magdalene could pass a whole evening quietly at the feet of Jesus, listening to His voice. A bride does not speak when her lips are covered with the kisses of the bridegroom.

The silent no longer need to worry about building on a rock. They become rocks on which others can build.

As the lotus, rooted in watery darkness, seeks the light and rises to the surface, so the silent, though born and educated in the world, rise above it in unsullied beauty.

St. Francis of Assisi went to town once with another friar to preach. On the way, they were mocked but did not reply. When they returned to the monastery, Francis asked the brother, "How did you like my sermon?"

"You did not say a word."

"We have both preached well," responded Francis. "The message of our sermons was to remain silent when scorned."

Historians report that when King Frederic II asked St. Francis why he was silent, he replied, "Who can put into words the sublimity of silent service?"

How can a God "with whom there is no variation or shadow of turning" (Jas. 1:17) move the whole universe? Only a motor that moves can move a machine.

Let a beautiful girl enter a room and sit down quietly in a chair, and all around her will begin to move. Beauty moves while remaining unmoved. God's splendor moves the universe.

Jesus said to Matthew simply, "Follow Me," without providing any argument as to why Matthew should abandon his business and go after an unknown (see Mt. 9:9). The radiation of Jesus' spiritual beauty was sufficient to impel him. Matthew locked his customs office and followed Jesus.

We do not need much talking and moving in prayer. Silent prayer imparts something of Heaven's glory. As we reflect the beauty of holiness, it will move God, Christ, the glorified saints, angels, and those in this world, without our pronouncing a word.

The jewel of silence is a pearl lost by the Church. Let us practice silence—but at the same time keep silent about the practice.

* * *

The English translation of Psalm 109:4 says, "I give myself to prayer." The Hebrew original contains only two words: "I—prayer," not even "I *am* prayer," which would establish a relationship between myself and prayer. This would overstate the meaning. I and prayer are identical, as Richard Wurmbrand and myself are identical.

Prayer should consist not only of words but also the spirit and the whole person. Augustine wrote, "The spirit prays, even when the tongue is silent," just as the heart and the kidneys function without speaking.

The essence of prayer is quietness, as the beginning of the Orthodox liturgy suggests: "Let us put aside all worldly worry." It is prayer to forsake my opinions, my fantasy, my passions, even my thoughts about God.

When my son was four, I told him to think about God. He replied, "Why should I think about this big God with my small mind? Let Him with His big mind think about me." Jesus said, "The Son of Man is coming at an hour you do not think…" (Mt. 24:44 NAS). Our thoughts play a secondary role in prayer.

At the entrance of a church in Albania, there was this inscription: "Those who wish to enter through the gate of God's house, leave the drunkenness of thoughts to find inside the Judge full of grace."

May prayer be an hour of secret communion with God, but not an hour of self-condemnation (of "down-thinking of yourself," as the Greek in First John 3:21 suggests).

Certainly it is proper to review in prayer your past sins one by one, but not as sins attributable to you. They belong to Jesus.

Luther wrote with much boldness, "Christ is the greatest liar, thief, murderer the world has ever had. Not through committing these deeds, but because He took them all upon Himself. Now they are His. After you have ascertained that, because of His sacrifice, you do not have any more sins, which now lie on His shoulders, meditate slowly on all His attributes, visualizing them not as His, but as yours, because they are His gifts to you. His splendid kingdom is within us."

Emerging from such an hour of prayer, you will be able to sing, whatever others may think, "I am a rose of Sharon" (see Song 2:1); "I am lovely" (see Song 1:5); "I will praise You, for I am fearfully and wonderfully made" (Ps. 139:14).

* * *

It is not the length of prayer that counts, but its quality. Many believers are sad because they feel they cannot pray much. If that is the case and no words come during your time of prayer, keep silent. Perhaps the Lord does not wish to have words. Do not lakes and forests speak to the human soul, though they have no mouth?

Contemplate the beauty of His holiness and meditate on His mercy and loving-kindness. What counts in prayer is above all the state of the heart.

* * *

I wish to have the truth for myself. There exists something better than this: It is the denial of self. Jesus teaches men to deny themselves for the simple reason that even without our denial, the self is only an illusion. It is we who gather on a string different events of our life, different opinions and convictions that we have maintained over time, and then designate them as the "self."

I am surely not my self. If I were to meet my self on the street as I was at the age of 9, or 14, or 30, or 50, I would not salute him. I would probably not recognize him, except that now we have photographs to remind us of what we once were.

If I were to read or hear the things I said when I was a child, a teenager, or a mature man before my conversion, I would feel absolutely no sympathy for those opinions. I would not even recognize them as being my own.

From Heaven's viewpoint the words and opinions of even the greatest saints on earth must seem childish; glorified saints would probably not recognize them as ever having been their opinion.

Jesus did not consider it useful for us to know even one of His thoughts or words between the ages of twelve and thirty. Of how much less value are our opinions!

What kind of self, then, can I boast of if I can detach myself from it; if I can deny it; or if I can even commit suicide?

Everything I observe has an objective existence: It can also be observed by other individuals, and I can verify my conclusions. The self can be contemplated by no one but me. I have no witness to corroborate my analyses. My "self" declares what my "self" is, and this "self" is not reliable.

Again, the self has as its material tool the brain. The brain is an apparatus with which we think that we think. But let us be honest with ourselves: How many hours a day do we use our brains for thinking? How much of what we have thought proves to be true?

A false comparison has been made between the human brain and a computer. The computer gives mathematically exact results; the brain does not. The self is a deceiver.

The self is a poor instrument for discovering truth.

* * *

The shortest biblical names of God in Hebrew are *Yah* and *El*. These names are found even in pre-biblical times, in the Ebla tablets.

It is said that the Japanese used to have very long names. By way of illustration, the story is told about a Japanese boy who fell into a well. Another boy desperately tried to explain to an adult that *Taramcecapatostarnecaton* was in danger of drowning, but by the time he finished saying the name, the boy in the well went down for the third time and was beyond saving. Ever since then, the story goes, the Japanese have restricted themselves to short names.

In Hebrew, the name *Yah* is constituted of only two letters. By pronouncing just one syllable, a person may be in His presence immediately.

America's fiftieth state, the Hawaiian Islands, were once called the Sandwich Islands after the Earl of Sandwich. From him also comes the name of a popular food often eaten between meals. A passionate gambler, he would not leave the gaming table for lunch or dinner. Therefore, he invented the "sandwich," which one can eat while pursuing other interests.

If a passion for gambling can shorten the time for eating, so a passion for Heaven may shorten religious talk, and what good is it anyway? "For whoever calls upon the name of the Lord shall be saved" (Rom. 10:13). For this purpose, God gives Himself— even in English—a monosyllable as a name and puts in one short word the single condition of salvation: "The just shall live by *faith*" (Rom. 1:17b).

* * *

The truth must also have a short name by which to be known to those who need it immediately. Like a coin or a bill hidden in a wallet, it must be readily available in an emergency.

But just as popularized science is not science itself, so a shortened message about the truth is not the whole truth.

Be happy to have found the truth in a short name and in a short message. Then seek diligently for more treasure when the emergency has passed.

Small nuggets of truth can tell us a great deal about the whole truth; but the whole truth, arrived at by conclusions from the few things that are known, must be kept entire. Nothing less than the whole creed will do in religious matters.

There is both an advantage and a disadvantage to short messages.

* * *

Suffering may help one to arrive at truth. "Tears, tears, bitter hulls but with such a sweet kernel," wrote the much-persecuted Romanian Christian poet, Traian Dorz.

Most people have an unjustified phobia against suffering. Unnecessary tragedy should be avoided, but we should also realize that there is much good in suffering.

Milton wrote his finest poetry after he became blind. Beethoven composed his most beautiful music only after he became deaf.

The German philosopher Kant, who suffered from an incurable sickness, wrote, "I have become master of its influence on my thoughts and actions by turning my attention away from this feeling altogether, just as if it did not at all concern me." William Wilberforce, hero of the fight against slavery in the British empire, could not live one day without pain-relieving drugs, but he had the willpower to take only a minimum dose.

Henry Stanley, reared in a poor children's orphanage, learned there the endurance he later needed to find the lost Livingstone and to explore the interior of Africa. Kernahan, born without arms or legs, became a member of the British parliament.

Solzhenitsyn wrote, "Blessed be thou, prison." The seven years he spent in Soviet jails made of him the most powerful opponent of Communism.

I can say about myself that my fourteen years in Communist prisons were the most fruitful years of my life.

I know of no great character formed apart from suffering. A world without suffering would consist of weaklings. What kind of love endures without painful sacrifice? He who counts the sufferings involved will never be a daring hero.

Jesus Himself was made perfect through sufferings (Heb. 2:10).

When Pope Alexander VI, criticized by Savonarola for his unworthy life, offered him the position of cardinal in order to keep him silent, Savonarola answered, "May God keep me from being unfaithful to Him. I do not desire any other red cap than the crown of a martyr colored with my own blood."

The highest state of a Christian reader, as well as that of a Christian writer, is to be Christ-like. (The reader who is not a Christian would please God by becoming one.)

Christ was called a "Man of sorrows" (Is. 53:3) and "the Lamb slain before the foundation of the world" (Rev. 13:8).

To be a Christian, whether writer or reader, means to become a co-sufferer with Christ. The more of His pain we are ready to share, the more truth we will receive.

Someday we will sit with Jesus and the Father on the heavenly throne from which universes are created and administered (Rev. 3:21). A merciful God "will wipe away all tears" from the eyes of His saints, and all will be able to rejoice wholeheartedly (see Rev. 7:17; 21:4).

* * *

This book claims to contain the truth, "the oracles of God." There exists a justified skepticism regarding the truth.

Anyone who is convinced that he has what he believes to be the truth must first believe that mankind can know truth and that mankind can know the means for discovering it. He must also believe that he personally knows these methods and has used them well.

Whoever is aware of the limitations of these conditions will not lightly assert that he has the truth.

Goethe said in a conversation with Luden, "Truth is something which must necessarily be thought; something which simply cannot be thought otherwise." An example would be that two and two are four.

The most widespread definition of truth is this: "correspondence between thinking and reality." But the question remains: what is reality? Does reality reveal itself to me as it is?

The world, including our bodies, is constituted of atoms, yet for centuries we did not know this. Who can count the multitude of other specks of reality hidden from us? Our thinking might correspond to reality as we know it today and still be very far from the truth.

To know a truth, we must first have a true definition of truth. I must know what truth is before I declare or accept a teaching as truth. I would also have to know truth before accepting as true any definition of truth. We therefore need an endless series of preliminary knowledge which is unrealizable.

Philosophically, truth is unattainable, but that is no cause for worry because mining is also philosophically impossible. For mining we need tools of iron. In order to have iron tools, we must first be able to mine for iron. And so the argument runs. Meanwhile, miners mine.

Chapter 5

The Cost of Truth

Jesus, referring to Himself, promised, "You shall know the truth" (Jn. 8:32). As a seeker for truth, one must fulfill certain conditions. The first is a readiness to suffer for it when it is discovered.

Four girls once met, whose names were Fire, Air, Water, and Truth. They spoke about many things. On parting, they said, "We are so happy together, let us meet again. Where can we meet? Fire, where do you live?"

Fire replied, "Sisters, rub two pieces of wood together and you will find me."

Air said, "You will find me wherever you see a flower trembling or a leaf moving."

Water said, "Dig in the earth at the roots of trees. I will be there."

Truth said, "I was expelled from the world and no one receives me. Whoever takes my side is crucified."

It is said that when Pythagoras discovered his renowned theorem, he sacrificed a hundred oxen to the gods. Then the legend states that all the oxen in the world tremble every time a truth is discovered, and the possessors of oxen kill the possessors of truth. Fearing this fate, most men settle for less than truth.

Not so Jesus. He said, "For this cause I was born, and for this cause I have come into the world, that I should bear witness to the truth" (Jn. 18:37). He witnesses to the truth and teaches us, by His example, to do the same whatever the result, even if it is a painful and shameful death on a cross.

Second, we must seek the true truth and reject any surrogate. A man went into a shop to buy cloth for a suit. He noticed that the shopkeeper's yardstick was short and asked him why. The merchant answered, "It doesn't matter. It may be short, but it's very thick."

Sometimes what is presented as truth might be very beautiful, attractive, or pleasant, and it might give peace or joy, but these qualities cannot replace the most important element we must seek in a religious teaching—its truthfulness.

Third, we must be very careful to examine the words and fruits of those who speak in the name of God. Credulity is dangerous. We can be led astray and lose our souls.

It is said that when Alexander the Great went to war against Darius, King of the Persians, he took a bath and caught cold. His friend Philip, a physician, cared for him. Just at that time, Alexander received a letter from his most faithful commander advising him to be suspicious of Philip and not to take his medicine because the physician was in collusion with King Darius to poison him. Philip had allegedly received money and the promise of Darius' sister for his wife. When the physician entered the room with his medicine, Alexander took the glass in one hand and with the other gave the letter to Philip. The emperor drank while Philip read. Then Alexander said to him, "I have confidence in your medicine and in your friendship." He regained his health.

This example is often quoted in sermons to suggest that if we can have such confidence in man, then we can have even more in God—our greatest Friend.

It is my firm conviction that, assuming Alexander really responded in this manner and the story is not legend, he was misguided. Many kings and rulers have been poisoned by their physicians. Many of Stalin's comrades were killed in this manner.

Jesus taught, "Beware of men" (Mt. 10:17). We must beware of men in material things, financial matters, and everyday affairs. Even more, we must not easily give our confidence when the eternal destiny of the soul is at stake.

If anyone desires salvation and sanctification, he might find a religious teacher who is trusted with speaking the oracles of God, but be very choosy.

* * *

One of Romania's richest men told me how he attained his wealth. At ten, he was a poor orphan boy without any income or possibility of schooling. He thought to himself, "What should I do? I can start to sell doughnuts on street corners. Then I will have doughnuts. If I start with gold, I will have gold."

He had seen a sign on a large building designating it as the seat of a gold-mining company, so he applied for the job of elevator boy. Once, the owner of the company rode up the elevator and asked who he was. He told his story including his motivation for applying at a gold-mining company.

The owner, impressed, called him into his office where he questioned him at length. He helped him obtain his schooling and enter the university. Eventually, he gave him his daughter as a wife and made him the heir of the company. This is how he became rich.

Dream big, think big. Old Testament Joseph, a shepherd boy, dreamed he would become something big and that his brothers, and even the sun, moon, and stars, would bow before him. His dreams may have seemed laughable, as yours will seem. But he became prime minister of Egypt, a benefactor to many people and a type of the Messiah to come.

I was a prisoner of the Communists, confined in an underground cell, but I dreamed about a world-wide mission. My dream came true. This Christian mission (The Voice of the Martyrs) now works in over fifty countries, Communist, former Communist and Muslim, and it prints Christian books in over sixty languages.

Expect great things from God and you will do great things for Him. They might not be spectacular in the eyes of others. Your works might not even be external. They may consist of forming a Christ-like character, rearing a child in the fear of the Lord, witnessing in humility for the Lord; but the results will be of eternal value.

Jesus said, "I will make you fishers of men" (Mt. 4:19). The first Christians used a fish as their sign of recognition because the Greek word for fish spells the initials of "Jesus Christ, Son of God, Savior"—*Iesus Christos Theos Hiou Soter.*

Yes, catch fish. Catch first of all the greatest fish, ICHTYS, Jesus Himself. When you have caught Him, you have caught the Truth itself, the most reliable of teachers.

* * *

A king asked several sages, "How is it that an aquarium filled with water and containing a goldfish weighs as much as the same aquarium with the same amount of water but without the goldfish?" Innumerable answers were given. Even the principle of Archimedes was quoted until in the end someone said, "But does this equality of weight exist? We should first check." Such individuals are rare.

Truth is not easily found. One would be well advised to beware of the peddlers of cheap truth, who rely on the immense credulity of people.

A story is told that may not be true, but it is an excellent illustration of man's gullibility. Allegedly, someone opened a restaurant but without much success. In danger of failing in his venture, the owner resorted to a device to attract customers. He put in the shop window an aquarium filled with water and an inscription, "Here are invisible fish." Thousands gathered to see the unusual fish, and business prospered.

Lord Boyd-Carpenter, who had been financial secretary of the British government under Churchill, wrote: "Once a gathering of the Defense Committee seemed to go on endlessly, without any progress. Churchill, getting bored, suddenly pointed a finger at the window and asked those present, 'What kind of bird is that?' Everybody stared at the window. One said, 'Probably a jay.' Another, 'Perhaps a sea gull.' And so on. Only one dared to say, 'I didn't see any bird.' To which Churchill replied, with laughter, 'There was none.'" In this simple way, he showed the ministers and the generals that they spoke empty words.

Likewise, in your search for truth, be sure you verify facts and challenge assertions before accepting them—especially if they ring true. No one likes to discover his coins are counterfeit. "Test all things; hold fast what is good" (1 Thess. 5:21).

* * *

In a renowned French movie, *Typhoon in Nagasaki*, a woman who loves an engineer named Morsac unexpectedly appears on the same train as her dear one who is leaving for Japan. Surprised, he asks, "Why are you here?" She answers, "I didn't stop to think even for a minute. If you leave, I leave too." He then kisses her and tells her, "How beautiful you are when you don't think."

In the Bible it is written that the Son of Man comes in an hour when we do not think (Mt. 24:44).

A converted lady who had once been an alcoholic was asked by what method she had overcome her addiction. She replied, "Method? Method takes thinking and repeated endeavors. I knew that my Beloved who died for me willed it, so I promptly obeyed. That was all."

The believer places himself before God like a canvas awaiting a painter. Obedience is taken for granted. The canvas, after all, does not resist the gentle pressure of the artist's brush.

The Christian life is not a life of constant choices between the ways of Christ and those of the world. We are living His life. The choice has already been made. Our self has merged with His Self. We are one in the Beloved who is the Truth.

* * *

A soldier by the name of Alexander was brought before Alexander the Great, charged with desertion. Hearing the accusation, the emperor said, "I do not punish you for your cowardice but because, as a man who trembles in battle, you bear my name and put it to shame. You would have gone free if you had changed your name."

We are sinners because, while bearing the name of Christ, we have not behaved accordingly.

After the fall, Jesus never had to choose between coming to earth and not coming. How beautiful that He did not stop to think. Let us imitate Him in this.

The Hindu, the Buddhist, and the Tibetan religions prescribe lengthy and difficult practices of meditation. Christianity is a natural daily loving fulfillment of the wishes of our Bridegroom.

* * *

In Carl Maria von Weber's operetta *Abu Hassan*, a man of Baghdad lived in utter poverty with his wife Fatima. In their desperation, they conceived of the idea that Hassan would feign death for, according to an old custom, every widow or widower without means would receive a big purse from the caliph for the burial. So Fatima ran to the palace with the false news and received a full purse from Zobeide, the caliph's wife.

Hassan then decided on another trick. Now Fatima would feign death. He ran to the palace and also received a purse, this time from the king. A quarrel arose between the caliph and his wife: Who died first, Hassan or Fatima? They went to the poor cottage and disputed the matter in the presence of the two would-be corpses. With a rising voice, the caliph finally promised loudly a thousand ducats to anyone who could tell him who died first. Immediately, Hassan revived and declared he was the first to "die" and claimed this money as well.

We too are poor creatures who have heard that God is rich in mercy toward those dead in trespasses and sins. He offers them forgiveness, blessings, and an eternal paradise.

Now, from this knowledge about the grace of God, two conclusions can be drawn: 1) we should endeavor to be gracious like Him toward those who sin against us, and 2) we should recognize that we are dead in sins without any possibility of helping ourselves, in order to obtain without cost, God's free gifts.

Once we have acknowledged that we are sinners by nature and can receive new life only through God's favor, we should not continue to feign death after being revived. We should not stretch out on a couch and let God do everything. Once you are alive, says St. Paul, "work out your own salvation with fear and trembling" (Phil. 2:12).

If Baghdad has a good caliph, he should be approached only in times of real need, not in place of working honestly for a living.

Similarly, it is not right to expect God to give us what we can obtain by our own endeavors.

* * *

Jesus said to the community of His disciples, "You are the light of the world" (Mt. 5:14). You are *one* light, not lights.

In the former West Germany one evening, 22 planes took off from a military airport for an exercise. Unexpectedly, a thick fog arose. Eight planes immediately returned to base. Four planes got lost. The pilots of the other planes tried to break through the thick wall of fog.

The local radio station interrupted its programming for an urgent news release: "All drivers are asked to go quickly to the airport and keep their headlights on. They will help the planes that are still lost in the fog to land securely. Please communicate the message to other drivers."

Soon the airport was surrounded by 2,500 cars. The drivers were ordered to turn their lights on bright. The lights of one car would not have helped the pilots, but thousands of massed lights did.

A fool poured a cup of water on a house that was on fire and then said, "You see, it is just superstition to believe that water quenches fire. I poured water on the fire, but it continues to burn." He was right, of course. One cup of water will not save a house on fire, but the combined mass of water in fire hoses can.

No one self has all the truth, but only the community of Christians. Let us unite our efforts. We will be able to serve as light to the world and to quench many fires from hell.

* * *

Ulrich Zwingli was a Catholic priest in Switzerland in the sixteenth century. A personal conversion experience led him to become first an adherent of Erasmus of Rotterdam and then of the reformer Luther. As a result of his influence, the Reformation became law in Zurich.

Many real abuses practiced in the Catholic church were abolished. All images and organs were thrown out of churches, and celibacy in the priesthood was renounced.

He had to fight at the same time on many fronts: against those who did not accept his puritanical morals, against the Baptists who did not recognize infant baptism, which Zwingli endorsed, and then also against Luther with whom he differed in the understanding of the Lord's Supper. Whereas Luther believed in "consubstantiation" (the bread and wine given to the communicant are the flesh and blood of Jesus), Zwingli believed that communion had only symbolic significance. Because of this difference, Luther refused even to shake hands with him.

Zwingli was very adamant about making the whole of Switzerland forcibly Protestant and urged the "slaughter of the Catholic cantons." He even used terror to encourage respect for his moral rules. In the end, he planned the blockade of food for the Catholic cantons that, with the support of Catholic Austria, then went to war against Zurich. The battle was fierce and hundreds died. The Catholics shouted, "Death to the heretics!" The Protestants replied, "Death to the idolaters!"

Catholics found the dying Zwingli and asked him if he wanted a priest. He made the sign "no." Then they told him, "There is no more time for confessing. Pray to the mother of God and the saints that they may obtain grace for you." When he refused this too, they decided he did not deserve to live.

After he was killed, opinions differed as to what to do with his body. Some proposed that he be cut in five pieces, one for each canton as a trophy. Others were for burning the corpse.

As for his master Luther, he considered Zwingli's death a judgment of God and wondered if the Swiss reformer could be saved and enter Heaven—not because he fought Catholics, but because he had committed the greater sin of differing with Luther on an understanding of Holy Communion. Yet Jesus, in instituting the Lord's Supper, said "Take and eat," not "Take and philosophize about it."

Jesus also said, "By this shall all men know that ye are My disciples, if ye have love one to another," (Jn. 13:35 KJV). We should all be ashamed of our past hostilities and the continuation of divisions. Let us be known by our love in spite of differences in opinions. It is clear that any opinion is no more than an opinion, not the truth. The truth is far above opinions.

* * *

On one point all large Christian denominations agree. The Catholics phrase it this way: *"Extra ecclesiam nulla salus"*—"Outside the Church there is no salvation." Calvin wrote, "Outside the church there is no forgiveness of sins, and you cannot hope for salvation. Abandoning the church is always fatal." Luther said the same: "Outside the Christian church there is no truth, no Christ, no salvation." These statements are of no great help because the question remains: Which is the Church?

The Jews had a church established by God Himself in all its details, yet its leaders consulted on how to kill the Messiah. "All the chief priests and elders...took counsel," (see Mt. 27:1). We are told this because the decision did not arise out of personal wickedness, but out of the collective wickedness of the social category to which the ecclesiastical judges belonged, what we term the clergy.

I would advise all seminarians and all students in Bible schools to show great diffidence and take many precautions before they seek to become part of the clergy.

In Matthew 23, Jesus pronounced an eightfold "Woe" over the Pharisees, the religious leaders of His day. He called them "fools and blind"; "hypocrites"; "serpents"; and a "brood of vipers."

Many consider these denunciations too violent and undiscriminating, but they were right.

The Lord does not denounce the existence of scribes or an ecclesiastical authority. But if we honestly view the characteristic vices of the clerical elite throughout the ages, especially when the Church was politically powerful, and their awful hindrance to the kind of spirituality Jesus taught, we are forced to acknowledge that He had good reason to utter these terrible woes.

Surely they can be read by the clergy—as well as the flock—only with a sense of horror, especially since the tragic history of the Church has shown the Christian clergy to be no better than the Jewish hierarchy. But why should men of God be so unreliable in spiritual matters? The reasons are many. I will name just one: The manner of recruiting clergy.

The Lord spoke to Moses, saying, ..."No man...who has any defect, may approach to offer the bread of his God, ...a man blind or lame, who has a marred face or any limb too long, a man who has a broken foot or broken hand, or is a hunchback or a dwarf, or a man who has a defect in his eye, or eczema or scab, or is a eunuch," (Leviticus 21:16-20).

The Jews in Jesus' time observed such commands punctiliously. In our day there are probably few Christian clergymen with such defects, but we have not delved into the deeper meaning of such words.

Why could a man with a broken leg not be a priest? It is because all men with deformities are in danger of developing an inferiority complex and therefore of over-compensating.

God desires that His servants not have defects in their spiritual body. A minister must have the right proportions; he must walk uprightly; he must grow to a proper stature and be full of courage; he must see well spiritually. No one should be ordained in a church without the healing of his spiritual infirmities. Then he will be able to impart truth.

* * *

In a factory where fine linen was produced, the workers were told to push a button if the threads became tangled so that the master could come to correct the work.

The threads at a machine where a young girl was working became tangled. An elderly co-worker came to her rescue, but she tangled the threads even more. When the master came, she apologized, "I did the best I could." The master answered, "The best thing you could have done was to call me in the beginning."

Mary Magdalene did not try to do anything. She just sat quietly at Jesus' feet and the tangled threads of her life were put in order. God said to Moses, "Tell the people to stand still." When they did, the waters of the Red Sea parted.

We must be like men possessing nothing, poor people following the poor Master in perfect quietness.

The earnest searchers for truth are strangers and pilgrims in this world, dead to its allurements and achievements. Expecting nothing from the world, they seek the truth, they love its message and revel in its beauty.

One of the conditions for obtaining truth is not to have possessions, and not to desire to have them. Jesus said, "Blessed are the poor" (Mt. 5:3). In Hebrew, the verb "to have" does not exist. You cannot say, "I have a house," "I have a car," because there is no concept of "having."

No one can speak the oracles of God, nor can one understand them, if he is attached to possessions.

When St. Francis of Assisi was converted, he threw his purple vestments and all his gold at his father's feet. Standing naked before him, he said, "I will no longer say, 'My father, Peter Bernardone' but, 'Our Father which art in heaven.' "

Because he had the truth, the prophet Jeremiah was taken prisoner and thrown into a muddy pit. He was not success-oriented though he spoke with great earnestness. He was content to fulfill his task, even while knowing his warnings would not be heeded. "Success is not one of God's names," wrote the Jewish philosopher Martin Buber.

A battle over what the truth is rages constantly. In times of war, truth is the first casualty. Everyone engaged in battle proclaims what is profitable for his cause, even if it goes against the truth.

The seeker after truth, then, does not run after the advantages gained from knowing it, reading it, or proclaiming it. He is simply thirsty for truth for truth's sake.

Only when written in this sense and when read with such a spirit will this book be useful.

* * *

We can have full confidence in God, the Author of truth.

Hunter and Percy Mather, missionaries in Mongolia, were lost in the Gobi Desert and could not find their way out. One day their servant came to them and announced, "We have only two handfuls of rice."

Mather answered, "It is not so." We have two handfuls of rice and God." And he sat down and recited Psalm 23, knowing that in difficult or depressing situations, God can introduce entirely new elements to alter circumstances. When he came to the words, "You prepare a table before me...," he looked up and saw the caravan of an English explorer who was passing through this inhospitable wilderness for the first time. The Englishman gave the missionaries all they needed and brought them safely out of the desert.

The Mathers knew that it was not admissible to say, "Lord, Lord" and not do His will, neither is it admissible for God to call us "My child" and "My son" and not give us what we ask of Him. They had confidence that their prayers would be answered.

It is wise to be optimistic in one's thoughts and attitudes. In the Sermon on the Mount, Jesus teaches us to think about God as the good Father who feeds even the birds. Now, birds have their predators, but we are enjoined to think about how God provides for them and to consider ourselves of much greater value. Jesus also suggests that we contemplate the lilies of the field, which God clothes with beauty, though they soon fade and die. We are urged to see the beauty, not the dying. It was Jesus' desire that we apply this principle of sanctified optimism to our daily lives.

* * *

In a Laurel and Hardy movie, Hardy is sick and asks his friend to fetch him a doctor. When he returns with a veterinarian, an indignant Hardy asks, "Why did you bring me a vet?" Laurel replies, "It is wrong to discriminate. A person's religion shouldn't count when you're sick."

This is only a comedy, you say. But for a great many people it just does not matter what religion they have, provided they have one. They are less choosy about religion than about food or clothes.

Religion shows me the way to Heaven, just as mathematics charts the course of a spacecraft. A small error in calculation and the astronauts would not reach the moon, nor would they return.

Wrong religion might yield some satisfaction—but it might also land us in hell. Right religion is more important than right virtue. The astronauts must first be sure that everything has been done to ensure a safe return to earth. Then they can decide which virtues to exercise.

At a party, the question was asked, "If you were shipwrecked on a lonely island, what one book would you prefer to have?" One said, "Shakespeare." Another, thinking to show himself a profound believer, said, "The Bible." The smartest was the third: "I would like a book that would teach me how to build a boat to help me get back to the mainland." Right religion is just such a boat.

When St. Paul preached in Athens, he did not say one word against sin, but only against false religion. Likewise, the Books of Kings and Chronicles in the Bible categorize the Jewish kings not according to their economics or politics, but only according to their manner of worship.

Don't accept a veterinarian as your doctor. You are human.

* * *

Every author rejoices when he sees a good review of his book. After we die, God will read the book in which we have inscribed the reality of our lives and will reward us accordingly. It is important to know that we have the possibility of receiving honor and glory from our heavenly Father.

Events on this earth are recorded not only in time and space. When the Russian Communists imprisoned and killed writers and destroyed their literary works, the theologian Bulgakov wrote, "Manuscripts don't burn." There is another world that keeps "photocopies" of all things written on earth.

Over two thousand years ago some obscure Essene scribes in the Qumran community wrote books that remained sealed in jars hidden in caves until the mid-twentieth century. For century after century no one knew of their existence. Then one day an Arab boy found a jar that led to the discovery of the Dead Sea Scrolls that have so marvelously enriched our knowledge of the Bible.

We may feel that our lives have little value or impact. But the life apparently lost on earth will reappear in a new and greatly improved edition. Such a hope cleanses the soul.

Chapter 6

Receive Truth

The Bible says that Satan deceives the whole world (Rev. 12:9). Since we are in the world, this means that we can be deceived too. If I am obliged to seek the truth, I might fail as other very sincere seekers have failed. Wariness is an essential part of faith.

Truth is not a butter knife, but a surgeon's scalpel. One must be ready to accept the rigors of its cutting edge.

For example, it is a painful truth that religious as well as non-religious literature is afflicted with the virus of banality. Very often it makes no difference which religious book you read because they all say the same thing. Conversion stories are virtually identical. Read the first three pages of almost any book and you can usually predict, with little margin for error, the middle and the end. To the contrary, God is never banal.

The French painter Chirico exhibited a large canvas on which nothing was portrayed and entitled it "Void Space." I prefer this to canvases smeared with banalities.

In another art exhibit an empty canvas was shown with the title, "The Grazing Cow." When the painter was asked, "Where is the grass?" he said, "The cow has eaten it all up."

"And where is the cow."

"Why should the cow remain if it can no longer find grass?" was the reply.

There is more content in such mockery than in many of today's religious books. If you seek the truth, be prepared for entirely new ideas and be willing to count yourself among the very few who receive the truth. Be ready for the eventuality that you might even have to stand alone in defense of the truth.

Nowadays, many churches believe that the truth is arrived at by taking a poll (a good example is the question of the ordination of women), but truth cannot be replaced with public opinion polls. Voices should be weighed, not counted. We have to distinguish between facts and opinions.

When a journalist writes, "Such and such a house burned down," he states a fact. You can verify it by going to see the rubble and ashes. But when he writes, "The concert was bad," he expresses only an opinion. Are you sure you are accepting facts—or merely opinions?

Seek truth even if it comes from very unlikely sources. Occasionally, one can receive fragments of it from untruthful persons. Heaven sometimes speaks through the mouth of Hell. The Apostle John made special note in his gospel of the words of the Jewish high priest Caiaphas who spoke the truth about Jesus' sacrificing His life for the people (Jn. 11:49,50), though Caiaphas did not mean to serve the truth. His words were correct, even prophetic.

The seeker after truth may be obliged to give up the beaten path. In the words of Robert Frost, the American poet, he may need to choose "the road less traveled by."

Bacon was the first to speak out against preconceived ideas, against people who took things for granted because authorities like Aristotle and Socrates had uttered them. He introduced the inductive method, which asks us to step from facts to teachings, instead of the accepted deductive method, in which men judged the facts according to the teachings of philosophers of old—who might be wrong.

Jesus said, "I receive testimony from no man" (see Jn. 5:34). No man, apart from Jesus, is reliable enough for us to build the whole edifice of truth upon his sayings alone. Not even my own mind is good enough for that.

When Peter declared that Jesus was the Son of the living God, Jesus immediately explained to him that these thoughts did not come from Peter's own mind but were a revelation from God.

We have draped over our beds tight mosquito nets of systems, conventions, abstractions, simplifications, and superficialities. We are also victims of the media who always have a bias. They choose to be anti-this or pro-that and then fit the facts into their predetermined mold. If there is an important political upheaval, the appreciation of these very same facts may undergo a radical change and be given a new significance entirely.

When Hitler took over Germany, the whole history of the country as taught in the schools was changed. The Communists used the same tactics when they came to power. Khomeini did the same thing in Iran.

Too often, the mind does not allow the facts to speak for themselves. They are confined in a straitjacket of preconceptions. Open the gates of your mind to new ideas. Jesus said, "Put new wine into new wineskins" (see Mt. 9:17).

Schiller wrote to Körner, "It is disadvantageous to the creative activity of a soul when the intellect examines too closely the ideas that steam towards it. An idea, fantastic in isolation, might become important through the one which follows it."

Resolve that you will renounce all repugnance toward a new idea simply because it is new.

* * *

If you are a seeker for truth, give up any hope of a quiet life. Emerson wrote, "God offers to every man his choice between truth and repose. Take whichever you please, but you can never have both."

Seek the truth, not expecting anything for yourself. Remember also that the truth you find might be acceptable for a time but may prove to be insubstantial or unreliable later on.

Rembrandt is the only painter who left 90 self-portraits. He painted pitilessly the slow ruin of his own flesh. His times of skepticism and courage, melancholy and calm, appeared like a full confession before a priest. He also painted fancies about himself. He painted himself as a wealthy nobleman and a flamboyant cavalier. Though by 1640 he had become the most successful artist in Amsterdam, he knew this popularity would not last. So he painted his decline as well. After ten years, his popularity was fading. By 1652, he was bankrupt.

As you view the truth about yourself, be sincere in accepting it.

* * *

If one were to try to use Hebrew to write a book proving that man has only one life, he could not do it. In the language of the Bible, the word for life is *haim*, a plural. (All the plural substantives end in *-im*.) In Hebrew one can only say, "I have lives." To say "I have only one life" is impossible.

There is such a thing as the next life. It is next door to this present life. But we do not have to await death to understand it because faith brings a foretaste of the future into the present.

The renowned English evangelist Charles Spurgeon once asked a parishioner who was on his deathbed, "Will you go to Heaven when you die?"

"No," was the reply, to the dismay of Spurgeon.

"Have I then preached in vain? Don't you know that believers in Jesus go to Heaven at death?"

The dying man answered, "Let them do as they like. I know better. I don't go to Heaven when I die. I have already been in Heaven for thirty years."

In Tewin churchyard, Hertfordshire, England, there are four trees growing from one root. These trees have an interesting story. When Lady Anne Grimston was dying, she mocked religion, saying, "I shall not live again. It is as unlikely that I shall live again as that a tree will grow out of my body." She died and was laid in a strong marble tomb with tall iron railings to hold the masonry together. Somehow a young tree broke through the masonry and destroyed the walls of the tomb (*The Book of Knowledge*, Educational Books, London, 1921).

Atheists have a vague sense of eternal life. Pasternak, whom I have already quoted, was brought up in a godless environment, but in his renowned *Doctor Zhivago*, he circles around the problem of eternal life:

"So what will happen to your consciousness? **Your** consciousness, yours, not anyone else's. Well, what are **you**? There's the point. Let's try to find out. What is it about you that you have always known as yourself? What are you conscious of in yourself? Your kidneys? Your liver? Your blood vessels? No. However far back you go in your memory, it is always in some external, active manifestation of yourself that you come across your identity—in the work of your hands, in your family, in other people. And now listen carefully. You in others—this reflects your soul. This is what you are. This is what your consciousness has breathed and lived on and enjoyed throughout your life—your soul, your immortality, your life in others. And what now? You began in others and you will remain in others. And what does it matter to you if later on that is called your memory? And now one last point. There is nothing to fear. There is no such thing as death. Death has nothing to do with us...."

This is how much he knew about eternal life. We know more. In no way can we conceive now the depth, the height, the breadth, the duration of God's love for us. So we cannot imagine yet what awaits us in eternal life.

We will continue to live, but not only in the memory of others. Jesus promised, "To him who overcomes, I will grant to sit with Me on My throne, as I also overcame and sat down with My Father on His throne" (Rev. 3:21).

Jesus assures us that there is such a thing as a divine throne. And we can be with Him as real beings, in actuality, sitting in the place from which universes are created and ruled.

I realize that words are not the names of things but of our idea of things. The words above are surely only our idea of the things that will be. But what will be are "real things" that will give us unspeakable joy and a rich reward. Life will have meaning and fulfillment there in a way that we cannot even imagine here.

* * *

There exists eternal life with a Heaven and a hell. Many descriptions of them in the Bible are obviously figurative. For instance, Jesus says of a Jewish city, "And thou, Capernaum, which art exalted unto heaven, shalt be brought down to hell" (Mt. 11:23a KJV). Now, Capernaum has never been in Heaven; that was simply a manner of describing how greatly exalted the city was. But then the descent to hell must also be only a figure of speech. Whatever the interpretation, there exists a place or state of reward and one of punishment.

We have to accept the fact that some of us shall be damned. Should we pray that no one will be damned? If lice, rats, and disease viruses could pray, that is what they would pray for. Should we pray that guinea pigs not die? Then children must die because of the many sicknesses that can be conquered only through animal experimentation. It is better not to speculate too much about the future, but rather to beware of hell.

We must know about Heaven and hell. Pascal wrote, "The immortality of the soul interests us so much, so touches our lives, that whoever remains disinterested, indifferent to it, must have lost any sentiment."

We need to decide whether we desire to go to hell, the place where men are immobilized in utter selfishness, or to Heaven, the place of utter compassion, of those willing to sacrifice themselves for the good of anyone who suffers in God's great universe if there is the slightest chance to save him.

It is obvious that as long as beings suffer, there will be no possibility of joy for the compassionate except the joy of sharing suffering and trying to be of service. Heaven is a place of love.

The selfish person does not have to die; he is dead already. Those here who are heavenly-minded already have a piece of Heaven and will be in Heaven. Death cannot abolish their existence.

If we are on the way to Heaven, the idea of death should not obsess us. Charles Spurgeon said rightly, "Remember you are immortal until your work is done. If the Lord has more witness for you to bear, you will live to bear it. Who is he that can break the vessel which the Lord intends again to use?"

During World War II, a bomb blast destroyed the beautiful stained glass windows of a European cathedral. Nobody bothered the man who gathered up the tiny fragments. After two years of assiduous labor, the stained glass windows were as good as new and could again embellish the altar.

God can give beauty for ashes, the oil of joy for mourning over the loss of loved ones, and garments of praise for the spirit of heaviness (see Is. 61:3).

Everything that has been wrong in life can be mended. We have only to throw every sin into the fire of Jesus' love. Essentially, hell is also that within us that has refused the fire of love. What dooms us to hell is only the terrible sense of ownership that claims for itself even sin. Throw sin away in the right manner and in the right place, throw it upon Jesus, and you will find yourself in Heaven.

* * *

We do not have the choice simply to disappear at death. Sigmund Freud was right when he said, "Fundamentally, nobody believes in his own death." No one could live a day, no one could ever smile, if he were truly convinced that all sense of being in this world is only to prepare a tasty meal for worms in the grave.

Even the heathen philosopher Seneca (the Emperor Nero's advisor) had intimations of immortality, for he wrote, "As nine months in a mother's womb keeps and prepares us not for itself, but for a world to which we are alike conveyed as soon as we are able to breathe independently and survive in freedom, just so we mature during the interval from babyhood to old age for another birth. A new birth awaits us, new circumstances. The day you dread as your last is your birthday for eternity."

Life after death is contested, though without conviction, by those who have no life before death, *i.e.*, the quality of life that nothing can destroy, not even death. Most people live lives easily disturbed by minor incidents. How could they believe otherwise than that death will destroy it? Such individuals may vegetate or hibernate, but they do not really live.

Some look down on ascetics, who practice detachment from this life in order to prepare better for the next, but the detachment practiced by the unbeliever demands even greater renunciation and more rigorous effort, because he must detach himself from a fuller, richer life in the here and now.

How much did Napoleon renounce to retain his pride! His last thought was to keep his title as emperor, as evidenced by the fact that he himself wrote the announcement of his death: "The emperor of France, Napoleon I. Bonaparte, died on...1821 after a grave and long sickness." His adjutant had to fill in the date.

Marshal Ney, who was with Napoleon during the invasion of Russia, signed his last letter with the title "Duke of Moscow." Camille Cemoulins, one of the leaders of the French Revolution, asked that his tombstone bear the inscription, "Here rests a man who has great merit before France."

Who cares today about all the titles these men had? Students become bored simply having to study about them.

The great German poet Goethe, on the contrary, was always a believer in eternal life. In his last letter to Wilhelm Humboldt of March 20, 1832, two days before his death, he wrote: "The thought of death does not frighten me, because I know that our spirit is indestructible and immortal. It is like the sun. It only seems to us that it sets, when in truth it moves continually and shines always."

The French queen Marie Antoinette, beheaded during the Revolution, prayed to God in her last letter that her son might not think to avenge her death, and then she blessed the henchmen who performed the bloody deed.

We need to decide in advance in what spirit to die. We would do well not to wait until the last minute as did Voltaire, the cynical critic of the Church. Only a few hours before death he wrote, "I ardently implore God for forgiveness."

How many funerals have we attended? Some day others will attend my funeral. To prepare silently for a good death is the highest philosophy.

"In all you say, remember your end and you will never commit sin," (Apocryphal *Wisdom of Sirach* 7:36). Plato once said, "*Vera philosophia est meditatio morti.* [True philosophy is the meditation on death.]"

Savonarola said,

"O man, the devil plays chess with you all during your life and waits for the moment of death to call 'Checkmate!' Therefore be ready. Think well about your last move. If you win at this move, you have won all; if you lose, everything has been vain. To win at this last move means to win the battle for life. Therefore watch out for the checkmate that threatens you. Always think about death, because if you are not well prepared for this move, you lose all you obtained in this life."

* * *

Death is the opposite of life. Things contrary to each other provoke sentiments at opposite poles— but not so where love to God intervenes. We must not hate death because we love life, nor the contrary. We can love life as long as its prolongation is possible without abdication of Christian principles. We also love death, God's messenger who brings us to Him.

Paul writes, "For to me, to live is Christ, and to die is gain," (Phil. 1:21).

Thus the miracle has taken place that overthrows all psychological laws. We can have the same sentiment toward opposites. It would seem logical that one who loves a friend can only hate his enemy. Not so in Christianity. We love friends *and* enemies, just as Jesus did.

We do not avoid the thought of death. It does not frighten us any more than life does. We look death in the face, and because it draws nearer every moment of our lives, we earnestly avoid sin.

St. Dionysus said, "No one who delves into the essence of sin wishes to commit it." Take one minute before committing any sin and say to yourself, "It can send me to hell." Then visualize the suffering and the eternal separation from a loving God. You will not sin. Think about the beauty of Heaven that you can inherit by refraining from trespasses, and you will not sin.

Savonarola also illustrates:

"Look to the hare. When dogs pursue him, he zigzags while fleeing, to deceive the enemy, that the dogs might not catch him. He was taught to do this by nothing more than dread of the dogs. Just so, if you will think about hell as your enemy, you will not sin as you do now, but will learn to flee from it. And when you are tempted to do evil, you will say: 'Shall I lose heaven, where comfort is eternal, and go to hell where suffering is unceasing, for a little satisfaction, for a little faith, for a little property, all transitory?'

"The one who thinks seriously about death will also think about Heaven and hell. Then love for God and fear will enter the heart and these will lead toward doing good and avoiding evil.

"In the desire to beware of sin, we must have God's grace. Without it and without the light of faith no one can shield himself from sin, and therefore those who wish to live a good life and to keep themselves pure from sin must first ask God to give them light. Therefore, take this as the first rule; pray every day to God that he might give you His light.

"Christians must wear the glasses of death. *Qualis unusquisque est, talia et sibi videntur—* Man looks at things according to his disposition. In wrath, you see one way; in passion, in greed, in love, another. May death always be before our eyes.

"You who wish to enrich yourself through dishonest deals, remember death. Put on the glasses of death and say: In hell none of the things I have will help me. You who run after fame, remember that you will die. Put on the glasses of death and consider that all the honors of the world will profit you nothing if you enter into hell. Woman, if you have the desire for luxury, put on the glasses of death and see how not to suffer eternal condemnation because of it. Youth, when tempted to commit sin, put on the glasses of death, remember that you will have to die, and serve Christ with a pure heart and body. Adults, put on the glasses of death and you will find that they will be very useful for the fight against all temptations."

It is good spiritual exercise to visit cemeteries and the dying. Take a skull as an object of meditation, remembering that this is what your head will one day be like.

Remember the Bible verse, "Precious in the sight of the Lord is the death of His saints" (Ps. 116:15). Pursue righteousness, and then don't worry. Neither future events in our earthly lives nor death can reach us at a speed of more than sixty minutes an hour. If one is a saint, death is no longer hideous.

* * *

What separates us from God, what hinders us from becoming gods (Jn. 10:34), what makes death frightening is the power of sin.

In the museum of Naples one can see an old caricature: a butterfly holding reins put around the neck of a dragon. The illustration represents the philosopher Seneca, who tried to restrain through his philosophy the murderous passions of his disciple, the Emperor Nero.

Philosophy is powerless before passion. It does not restrain even the philosopher who himself is dominated by sin.

Evolution is impossible in any sphere without differentiation. Inequality is the motive force of the universe. Energy is manifested only where there is a difference of level. Therefore, as the laws of thermodynamics indicate, the difference between God and man had to exist, man of course being on the lower level. Sin is the stubbornness to remain at a low level.

Some people are free of certain sins. The individual who has never loved does not know the sin of jealousy. Those without the slightest bent for fantasy do not lie. The impotent do not commit adultery. But everyone fights sin of some kind and seems to do his best at times to put himself to shame.

Who could possibly enumerate all human sins?

* * *

The first man born on earth, Cain, was a murderer, but he could easily have found forgiveness.

Jewish legend says that Cain told the Lord, "Well, I killed my brother, but You are the one who put a bad impulse in me. You, the guardian of all creatures, allowed me to kill Abel. You are the one who killed him. If You had received my gift as You did his, envy would not have arisen in me. You must have informers around You because my father and my mother are here on earth and do not know that I killed Abel. But You are in heaven. How do You know it?"

The Lord said, "Fool, I carry the whole world. I made it and continue to carry it."

Cain said, "You bear the whole world and don't wish to bear my sin?"

God was in Jesus and bore the sin of the whole world, including the sin of Cain. But since the time of Cain, murder has never ceased.

In fact, sin has blighted the landscape of earth so that everything is tainted. By the time of Noah, God noted that "...the wickedness of man was great in the earth, and that every intent of the thoughts of his heart was only evil continually," (Gen. 6:5).

If the dollar bills that pass through our hands could tell their story, we would shun them. How many individuals have sold body and soul for this dollar, how often has it been used for alcohol, gambling, prostitution, for a bribe, or for weapons? It is soiled with tears and blood. No beverage inebriates like money.

How ugly is envy! Men snuff out big candles so that their little lights might be seen. A story is told about an angel who came to an envious man and told him, "God has decided to grant you whatever your heart desires, but only with the proviso that the competitor whom you envy will get double what you receive."

The man was granted 24 hours' time to think. Then he said to the angel, "Gouge out one of my eyes so that my competitor may lose all his sight."

Man is capable of many things. He can reach for the stars or sink to the level of a brute. He can use his gifts in the service of others, as Jesus demonstrated, or bury his talents in the ground, thus polluting mother earth. He can enter Heaven by faith or sink into hell by wickedness or indifference.

Heaven or hell—this is the choice. And it must be made.

* * *

Obviously, the intelligent choice is not to sin. Human effort can obtain much, even if not everything in this regard.

Greek mythology tells about the sirens—half woman, half bird—who sang songs in the Aegean Sea to entice sailors to abandon their ships and drown. Ulysses escaped the temptation by plugging his sailors' ears with wax and having himself lashed to the mast of his ship so that none of them could respond to the seductive sweetness.

Orpheus, too, passed those rocks where the sirens dwelled, but his method of escape was to play and sing with such surpassing sweetness that he drowned out the ravishing songs of the sirens and caused them to abandon their enterprise.

People today can plug their ears to the temptations of sin. They can refuse to read bad literature, watch bad movies, frequent bad places. They can sing a song more beautiful than the cheap songs of a sinful world.

But even the best succeed only partially. Most don't even try. Mankind is burdened with grave sins.

* * *

Individuals can repress remorse for a long time, though not forever. A man in Tennessee kept for nearly 70 years a secret that could have freed a Jewish factory superintendent who was convicted and later lynched for the murder of a fourteen-year-old girl. At the age of 83, Alonzo Mann signed a sworn affidavit naming a janitor at the factory and claiming that the star prosecution witness against the superintendent had threatened to kill him if he revealed the truth. His parents had also warned him not to get involved. Anti-Semitism, mob violence, and a revival of the Ku Klux Klan followed.

Everyone tries to run away from the memories of his sins, but they will entrap him, if not in this world, then in the next. We all need forgiveness, and we can have it without charge, with no strings attached. Jesus expressed the desire that those who are forgiven should in turn forgive others. But God forgives before we decide on what to do about those who have wronged us.

In *The Brothers Karamazov* by Dostoyevski, Ivan raises objections to forgiveness. The Soviet regime is filled with such unspeakable cruelty that people forget the horrors of the Tsarist regime. Dostoyevski tells about a Tsarist general from whose garden a child stole some apples. Incensed, he had the child stripped naked, then forced him to run and ordered dogs to give chase and tear him to pieces. Who would have condemned a Tsarist general?

Ivan says that God refuses even the Virgin Mary's prayers for the forgiveness of such wicked men until all their victims have forgiven them. How can the mother of this child forgive? The past event is irremediable. What has been done cannot be undone.

Ivan concludes:

"I don't desire that the mother embrace the wicked person who had her son torn by dogs. She should not dare to forgive. If she wishes, she might forgive him for herself; let her forgive the immeasurable pains of a mother; but she is not entitled to forgive the suffering of her child hounded to death. She, as a mother, is not allowed to forgive the wicked person even if the child itself has forgiven."

It is simple to deal with Ivan's objections. We all commit bad deeds in our dreams. We are not bothered by them when we awake. At the resurrection, we will realize that the world from which we have come was not the real world. The man I killed in dream is alive. The girl I polluted is pure. The man from whom I stole lost nothing.

So it will be when we encounter our former acquaintances in the other world. I will have done no one any wrong; on the contrary, I have done them good.

Jesus tells about a thief named Zacchaeus who had stolen from many people. He repented and restored fourfold what he had taken unjustly. The man who had lost $1,000 now had $4,000.

Jesus forgives because He is not only compassionate toward His martyred Church, but also full of understanding for the murderous general. He had been a child once and, like all children, had belonged to the Kingdom of Heaven, the kingdom of childish innocence. But He also had been badly treated by those in authority.

No one becomes a murderer just because he likes the idea. Circumstances bring some to this extremity. Even the Nazi and Communist murderers have, each of them, a story about how they became murderers.

A French proverb says, "Who understands all, forgives all." God understands everything. Therefore, everyone can obtain forgiveness.

Stalin was the illegitimate child of a nobleman, who bribed a drunkard, a cobbler, to marry his pregnant mistress. The story became known. As a child, therefore, Stalin was the object of mockery. Children teased him and called him a "bastard," at that time a very degrading appellation.

Then he went to a seminary run by the Russian church that was very chauvinistic. In the seminary of only Georgian students, the mother tongue was forbidden. Stalin was Georgian.

When Stalin was 15, his real father was killed, and he was accused of the murder. Because he was an illegitimate child, he was treated as one belonging to the lower class. For lack of sufficient evidence, he was acquitted.

He later became a member of the Social Democratic Party, as the Bolsheviks were then called. He was given the assignment to commit robberies in order the finance the party, while his comrades spent their time propagating ideas or organizing strikes against actual injustices. During this period, he fell in love with a girl, but then she was given the assignment to become the mistress of a rich man in order to get money from him for the party. The next day she hanged herself—and so on and on his story goes.

We surely deplore Stalin's cruelty toward his victims, but a knowledge of his background helps us understand his moral deviations and excesses. They can be forgiven, especially since we believe in a resurrection in which the innocent will be rewarded for what they suffered with love and faith.

The feelings of martyrs in Heaven must be ambivalent. They feel that their sufferings must be avenged (Rev. 6:9,10), but would they have had such shining crowns and the white garments of conquerors if it had not been for those who martyred them?

There is a place for forgiveness.

* * *

An important question was posed by Simon Wiesenthal in his book *The Sunflower*. Wiesenthal is a Jew who suffered persecution under the Nazis and afterwards dedicated his life to hunting those suspected of Nazi war crimes. (Why only Nazi war crimes? The Soviets and the Western allies also committed crimes.)

He had worked during World War II as a slave laborer in Poland doing repairs in a hospital. A nurse called him to the deathbed of a Nazi officer who, with great remorse, told him this story.

He confessed to Wiesenthal that he had been among those who crammed many Jews into a house together, including women and children. Inflammable canisters were set inside, and then the Nazis tossed in grenades that exploded, causing a conflagration.

An old Jew jumped from a window with a little child whose eyes he covered. His garments were aflame. This officer shot them both.

A few days later, he found himself on the battlefront with an order to attack. As the Russian soldiers advanced, he saw coming toward him the burning Jew and the child and said to himself, "I will not shoot at them the second time." In that moment a grenade exploded near him, mortally wounding him.

Before dying, he had only one desire that he had communicated to the nurse: a Jew should tell him he was forgiven. Wiesenthal heard the confession of the repentant Nazi officer but left the room in silence. He did not say "I forgive."

Since then over forty years have passed, but Wiesenthal has not found peace of heart. He goes from person to person asking, "Did I do right not to say a word of forgiveness? Had I the right to forgive in the name of the Jewish people?"—a question that could also be inverted: "Had I the right to refuse forgiveness in the name of the Jewish people?"

Should he have forgiven? Have the victims of this Nazi officer no right to be avenged, with at least the satisfaction of knowing that he would not die with the serenity of a forgiven man?

Can we be forgiven so easily for all our sins? Can God afford to be so nice? Can man?

Should a mother forgive the one who ordered dogs to maul her child to death? Is she authorized to do so? Who authorized her? The innocent child perhaps?

But again, who gives her the right to be cruel to the murderer and to refuse forgiveness? Does she know how the murdered child thinks about the matter in the next world where he is with Jesus? Jesus forgave those who crucified Him. Is it forbidden to be more than human, far beyond the usual run of men? Is it forbidden to be more than human, better than the best?

Rabbi Hillel advised that we judge no one until we have been in his situation. But have the innocent necessarily been in the situation of murderers or other kinds of vile sinners?

I prefer the attitude of Mrs. Rathenau to Wiesenthal's. Her husband had been a Jew and served as the finance minister of Germany in the twenties. An anti-Semite killed him only because he was Jewish. The mother of the murderer was in desperation over the crime her son had committed. Mrs. Rathenau, wife of the victim, a Christian herself, went to comfort her. She also visited the murderer in jail and brought him to Christ.

Many years later, the murderer was in a high command position in the German army in Marseille, during the Nazi occupation of France. He did his utmost to help Jews escape from France and thereby saved the lives of a great multitude. In the end he was discovered. The former anti-Semite murderer was executed for having been a savior of Jews.

* * *

Full forgiveness and forgetfulness of wrongs endured are both possible. Depth psychology asserts there is no forgetting, but only de-actualization. However, since through the new birth man becomes a new creature, the past is buried, never to be resurrected. Therefore, nothing divides a person from the one who has hurt him the most. Paul became a respected apostle in the community of early Christians, many of whom he had sentenced to death while persuading others to renounce their faith.

There can be no limit to forgiveness, just as there can be no degree of honesty or virginity. A girl cannot be half-pregnant. Forgiveness is total or it is not forgiveness.

The average man identifies with either the murderer or the victim. Christians can identify with both and love both. In my own case, I always pray for both parties.

The murderer, by killing, has broken a divine law: "Do not kill." Is this law an absolute? The same God ordered the extermination of the Canaanites and the execution of criminals. What if the young German SS officer had been taught to consider the Jews as reprehensible as the Jews in Joshua's time considered the Canaanites?

Why should it have been compulsory for the SS officer to obey the law against killing if we disregard another law of the same God that we must forgive those who trespass against us? The conscience of every person can err. There exist depths in men that attract some to crime, others to sainthood, depths that can also make a criminal become a saint (what every criminal becomes who contritely confesses his sins) and a saint a criminal that is beyond our comprehension. Since every man is a riddle to his fellow man, the best recourse is not to judge but to be helpful.

If Jews will not forgive the death of six million at the hands of the Nazis, neither should the blacks forgive the enslavement of millions who perished in slave hunts in Africa, and other millions brought to America by the slave-traders; Armenians and Greeks should not forget the Turkish massacres; Arabs should not forget their losses during the establishment of Israel; other nations should not forget the Communist mass murders; Protestants should not forgive the Catholics nor Catholics the Protestants; the North and the South should not forget the thousands who died in the fratricidal American Civil War; the Americans should not forget Bataan, nor the Japanese Hiroshima—one could multiply instances of cruelty and barbarism *ad nauseam*.

If no one could forgive and no one forget, where would we all be? Nations, religions, and alliances exist only through the grace of forgiving and forgetting even heinous crimes.

Spinoza once wrote cynically, "Everyone has as much right as he has might." Men may have the might to kill, but not the right. We recognize only the right to forgive and also to ask forgiveness.

Chapter 7

Endure the Pain of Truth

A legend says that Jesus was once seated at a banquet in Heaven with His apostles. One place was empty. Jesus had not yet pronounced the blessing, so no one had started eating. At a certain moment, Judas entered the room. Jesus received him as a friend and said, "I have waited for you. Now the meal can begin."

I dreamed one night that I asked Mussolini and some other dictators forgiveness for the fact that I do not have a yielding and humble character, that I do not do gladly what others demand of me and thus oblige them to dictate to me. In my dream, in the measure to which I asked forgiveness, the dictators ceased to exist. I find this dream very significant.

Jesus was modest in His demands but rich in His example. In the Sermon on the Mount, He spoke only about forgiving the one who gives you a slap, or takes away your coat, or compels you to do forced labor. But He Himself forgave Caiaphas, Pilate, and His executioners when He said on the cross, "Father, forgive them, for they know not what they do" (Lk. 23:34).

It is well to follow not only His words but also His example, perhaps even to surpass it, as He suggests in His matchless discourse at the Last Supper (Jn. 14:12). God is love. We must *be* love, not only exercise it.

* * *

I have known no believer who was not at some time or other troubled in his faith by the fact of pain. Why should a good God have ordained pain? "Pain is a more terrible lord of mankind than even death itself," wrote Albert Schweitzer.

However, we are told that the main function of pain is to signal the body of any harm to its tissues. We need such signals, admittedly, but could we not do with something less traumatic?

Experience has shown that what is not painful does not work. We do harm to our bodies with our smoking, drinking, poor eating habits, and promiscuity. We ourselves cause our own cancer and heart disease, but because we feel no pain before it is too late, we continue these suicidal practices. Pain is a sign of the intense desire of God to do us good.

If not for pain, we would undoubtedly disregard many dangers to the organism and would compromise ourselves still further. The inability to sense pain is one of the horrors of leprosy. But most of us see pain only as an enemy, and so we consume annually thousands of tons of pain-killers.

Muslims attribute pain to fate, Kismet; Hindus to karma, the result of sin in past incarnation; other Middle Easterners to the evil eye. Pain has meaning. By taking pills, our medicated society deprives itself of the discovery of meaning.

Pain can also be borne courageously; it can be faced. Societies that flee pain in all circumstances turn to horror movies and violence to compensate. Jesus at the cross refused an anesthetic.

Try the experiment of fixing a short time for bearing pain without an analgesic or sorrow without a tranquilizer. Remember that Rachel refused comfort (Mt. 2:18).

A man sleeping on the ground with his mouth open had a snake crawl down his throat. Another man who witnessed the event shook him awake and vigorously pounded him on the back again and again to make him vomit. The first man understandably resented what he considered an unjustified attack and responded violently. When finally he vomited up the snake, he had his explanation and complained, "Why didn't you tell me what you were doing?"

The reply was simple: "You were not receptive to arguments at that point. A person in that predicament needs a kick, not an explanation!"

If God permits suffering, we can be sure it is more painful for Him who permits it than for us who bear it. If we had His wisdom and sought our salvation as passionately as He seeks it for us, we would choose to pass through the very sufferings that afflict us. Therefore, believers bear with understanding the sufferings imposed upon them.

In *The Fathers of the Desert* appears the story of a monk well versed in fasting and asceticism who could not resist the thought of whoredom. With this in mind, he went to Jericho to fulfill his desires, but when he approached the prostitute, he discovered that he was covered with leprosy. Gratefully, he returned to the monastery praising God:" Glory be to Thee, O God, that You gave me this punishment to save my soul."

Some believers choose voluntary sufferings. In the *Zohar*, an ancient book of the Jewish *Kabbalah*, it is written, "Why did Jacob choose to work seven years for Rachel and not only a few months?" The reply is, "So that when at last he came to her, he would be as it were the Heaven to her earth."

Suffering works. Exile changed the Fascist dictator Mussolini into a Christian. Dostosyevski, sentenced to death in his youth and pardoned when he was already on the gallows, said that in the moment when he slipped from the noose around his neck, he had an illumination: "As an atheist I had been in prison even when I was free, but now jail has become for me the gate to freedom."

Dostoyevski remained sick for the rest of his life. God must have had a purpose in this because as a result he created works of art from the sickness of the world in his books *The Idiot, The Demons, Crime and Punishment*, and so on.

Someday we too may learn that there was a reason for the sufferings we have endured.

* * *

An artist painted a bad conscience as a galloping horse surrounded by wasps and mosquitoes. The caption read, "Your running is in vain."

Augustine said it in words, "A man bothered by his conscience is his own punishment. A man can run away from his enemies, but where can he find refuge from himself?"

Regrets alone do not help a troubled conscience. The mind that decides to sin then decides to regret, but conscience is not assuaged. Judas regretted profoundly that he had sold his Lord. Then the same mind reverted to despair and soon decided on suicide.

Repentance is something entirely different. In repentance, one ignores the mind that Luther called "the beast reason, whose eyes should be gouged out, the devil's bride, a lovely whore." He said to reason:

"Listen, you have lied to me often and in weighty matters in which it was not your business to interfere. You have a limited low-ranking job in matters which do not involve religion, morals, ultimate truth. Stick to your menial work. For overstepping your attributes, I give you the boot. Out! Henceforth, the mind of Christ will be my mind, I will not be taught anymore to sin, neither to lose my time in vain regrets, nor ever to despair."

This is the change that takes place at the new birth. With such an attitude, even after the betrayal, Judas would have been spared his tragic fate. Saul of Tarsus, the great persecutor of Christians who became the apostle Paul, is an example of what can happen to a person who truly repents.

If Judas had been born again after the betrayal, he would be known today as St. Judas Iscariot. He could have lived out his life and died with peace, understanding that he had been sacrificed on the altar of gathering precious experiences for the Church, just like the man who was born blind with all the ensuing suffering, for no other purpose than that "the works of God should be revealed in him" (Jn. 9:3).

* * *

Truth can be attained only by individuals who have been born again. No one who assumes false names and titles can be considered a gentleman. We bear the name of Christians. Are we entitled to it? Jesus said we must be born again. Have we passed through the new birth? Without this we are fake Christians.

Nothing except the new birth can enable us to get to Heaven. No amount of religiosity can cleanse us of our sins.

A Samaritan woman asked Jesus some theological questions. His response was, "Go get your husband and bring him here." The man whom she called her husband really belonged to another woman. And this was not her first sin. She had known many men, from whom she had received pleasure or money. Certainly she had not fulfilled the aim for which God brings individuals together—to help one another become like Him.

This woman did not need theology. She was lost. And it made no difference whether she worshiped according to the Samaritan or Jewish religion.

No good intention helps. If a person has ink on his fingers, his decision to wash himself will not make him clean. Only the act of washing removes the stain. We need the washing of the new birth. Therefore we extend to all people everywhere the warning, "You must be born again."

A man who was eating his lunch in a restaurant was approached by another man from a nearby table, who said, "Sir, may I tell you something?"

The first man replied, "I see by your face that you mean serious business. I want to enjoy my dinner, so kindly leave me alone." After finishing his ample meal, he turned to his neighbor: "I did not mean to be rude, but I was very hungry. Now you can tell me what you had on your mind."

The other responded, "I'm sorry, but it's too late. I only wanted to tell you that you had put your overcoat on a chair too near the stove. By now the heat has burned a large hole in it."

Most people do not wish to be disturbed by serious talk about what follows death and about the need for a new birth in order to enter Heaven. The loss is theirs! After death, they will have to face either Heaven or hell. And "unless one is born again, he cannot see the kingdom of God" (Jn. 3:3).

A monk always complained to his abbot about the evils committed by his brethren. Exasperated, the abbot advised him to go on a pilgrimage to Israel and bathe in the river Jordan. "But," he told the monk. "when you bathe, you should wear around your neck a garland of onions, garlic and green peppers." The monk returned from the pilgrimage but was still the same man, delighting in slandering others.

The abbot asked him, "Did you bathe in the Jordan?"

"Yes."

"Did you wear the garland of onions, garlic, and green peppers?"

"Yes, though I saw no sense in doing so."

"Please bite into the onion and the garlic." They were bad-tasting, strong and burned his mouth.

"Now bite into the pepper." The monk spat after having done so. Then the abbot said, "You see, bathing onions and peppers in the Jordan does not help. Neither do the rituals to which you subject yourself."

Nothing helps except becoming an entirely new creature who yields up all his self-will. The newborn man is compared by Jesus to the wind that blows in different directions, simply fulfilling the laws of its nature (Jn. 3:8).

Cromwell said, "The man who does not know where he is going, goes the farthest." The Bible asks, "Who is blind but My servant?" (Is. 42:19). Abraham forsook his surroundings to follow God to a country that would be shown to him. He was not told where it would be. The newborn man is like an object without its own will, like clay in the hands of the Divine Potter.

Before becoming a man, Jesus was a babe; and before that an embryo; before that a divinely fertilized ovum; before that "the holy thing" (Lk. 1:35); a conglomerate of molecules that needed to be organized into a living cell.

In First Corinthians 1:27, it is written that God chose not men, but certain "things" to be his representatives in the world, *i.e.,* men without self-will, like inanimate objects, ready to be used. This is the result of the new birth.

A kingdom was waiting to have Saul proclaimed as king, but he (unaware of the occasion) was seeking asses. The most beautiful kingdom, the kingdom of Heaven, is awaiting us, on condition of our being born again. Yet we run after trifles.

A king who had a rebellious son sent him into exile. As a result, the son suffered many years of deprivation and even hunger. In the end, the king had compassion on his son, forgave him, and sent emissaries to bring him back. Their instructions were, "Give him whatever he desires." When the prince saw them, he said only, "Give me something good to eat." He could have had his position in the palace restored to him, but he yearned only after a loaf of bread and butter.

We are all in the same situation. Through the new birth, we can become God's children, yet even when we talk with God's messengers, we settle for trivial things.

Express your desire for the new birth today and confess publicly that you belong to Christ. Then your natural desire to be thought consistent will enable you to follow through and investigate Jesus' teachings, and He will give you the grace of being born again.

* * *

God's great gift is the possibility of being born again. The new birth does more than purify from sin; it deifies men.

The newborn man begins to live and act as if he had seen paradise before his eyes. Then slowly the baptism of action drives away the dark clouds that veil Heaven, and as clearly as he sees material things, he gains the intuition of invisible powers because this invisible world will become real.

A newborn man is a man who has found God, and all at once the vague, distant notion of the Godhead is exchanged for a personal, sensible, present, and living reality. Here resides the distinction between repentance and regret.

My five-year-old grandson Alex, on being told that he had to go to the doctor's office, asked, "What for?"

"For the cough."

Later, he cheerfully reported to me, "They were wrong to take me to the doctor. He doesn't cough."

When we have sins, problems, and sorrows, pastors show us the way to Jesus, the great Physician. We return from Him radiant: "He is all right. He does not cough. He has none of our problems and unrest."

Jesus met a persecutor of Christians, a multiple murderer and blasphemer, on the road to Damascus. He asked Saul of Tarsus nothing about his state of mind. He did not examine him, X-ray him, inquire about what he had done, come up with a diagnosis, or give a prescription. Jesus simply revealed Himself in the glory of His resurrection. That was all. Then Saul knew, "The doctor does not cough. There is nothing wrong with Jesus. He is healthy, alive, powerful, loving. Far from telling me I must be hospitalized, He gives me great and noble tasks to perform."

This is the story when a soul has the privilege of meeting Jesus directly. But rarely does this happen. Usually, we meet Him through our Christian leaders and authors of religious books—all Christ's underlings. These surrogates do not always grasp the deep meaning of Jesus' parable of the lost sheep:

What man of you, having a hundred sheep, if loses one of them, does not leave the ninety-nine in the wilderness, and go after the one which is lost until he finds it? And when he has found it, he lays it on his shoulders, rejoicing. And when he comes home, he calls together his friends and neighbors, saying to them, "Rejoice with me, for I have found my sheep which was lost!" I say to you that likewise there will be more joy in heaven over one sinner who repents than over ninety-nine just persons who need no repentance (Luke 15:4-7).

When little Alex heard this story and was asked what he understood from it, he replied, "The shepherd should have been more careful not to lose the sheep."

Holding revival meetings over and over is not enough. In fact, why should Christian "patients" have to be revived at all? Once they are newborn in the faith, why should they get lost?

Luther, drastic as usual in his expressions, when asked, "Whom can we call a true Christian?" replied,

"Whoever has once entered a church. That nothing came of it is not his fault, but that of the pastor."

According to the apostle Paul, "God Himself gave some to be pastors and teachers" (Eph. 4:11). Why? If Christ is always with His Church, what is the purpose of subsidiary pastors?

One might as well ask why, when electricity is available everywhere, a lamp is needed to give light. Electricity has to have a focal point at which to manifest itself. The pastor is the focal point through whom Christ shows His beauty.

But the pastor should represent Christ faithfully. It is not enough for him to be a good pastor; he must be an excellent one. Observing him, people should be able to conclude, "the doctor does not cough. I don't have to worry."

A child was asked, "What is Sunday school for?" He replied, "To make children good so they can be resurrected." This is the pastor's occupation. He is a maker of saints, not a maker of sermons, and even less of money.

* * *

Who are the pastors one can trust? In 1179, at the third Lateran Council, the papacy decided to uproot heretics. As a result, the Albigenses, the Waldenses, and later the Hussites were tortured and killed by the thousands. Many were killed merely for possessing a Bible.

Pope Pius V was canonized, though the breviary calls him "the ruthless inquisitor." In the same breviary, the lesson for May 30 praised King Ferdinand II of Castile for his zeal against heretics. He himself, eager to perform good deeds, carried the wood for the stakes on which heretics were burned.

Ironically, the Protestant reformers often echoed the sentiments of the Catholics they opposed. Calvin wrote:

"We should define the power wherewith the priests of the church should be invested, seeing that they are put to administer, to proclaim and to preach the Divine Word. Their duty is to dare everything and to compel all the big and highly situated in this world to bow before the majesty of the Almighty God and to serve Him. It is given to them to command everyone from the highest to the most common. It is their duty to build the Kingdom of God and to destroy the wolves. They have to reprove and to give advice to those who listen; to accuse and to destroy the adversaries. They can bind and loose; they can throw lightning and thunder; but all these things in conformity with the Word of God."

Calvin meant just that. He too burned at the stake those with whom he disagreed. We cannot walk in the footsteps of Catholic inquisitors or Protestant persecutors. To whom then should we go?

Jesus said, "I will build my church." He used the future tense. He did not say when He would have a church worthy to be called His. Perhaps the churches of today are only the scaffolding for building that one church.

A few have recognized it and have already come to the "church of the firstborn who are registered in heaven" (Heb. 12:23). Seek this church! Seek it within the churches to which you belong!

At a certain moment Jesus gave to Simon a new name—Peter. His true name from then on was the one Jesus had given him, not the one he was known by. He thought of himself as Peter; the past of a certain Simon no longer belonged to him.

We too have to look upon ourselves as Jesus does. We have to call ourselves by the names He gave us: "children of God," "elect," "much beloved," and "apostles."

At a certain point, Simon declared, "I am something entirely different from what I have been. I am not Simon but Peter. When you call 'Simon,' I will not turn my head." If he were here today, he would probably change the name on his driver's license.

The whole world—as well as we ourselves—realizes we are a Church torn asunder by schisms and heresies, hostilities and iniquities, soiled by the blood of innocents shed by fellow Christians.

Neither are we what the world calls us, or what we ourselves think we are. After meeting Jesus, we were called His "fair bride," "a glorious church, not having spot or wrinkle, or any such thing" (Eph. 5:27). How is this possible? We simply become, through His transforming power, what He says we are, though the world may see us differently and we may have misgivings.

We are one because He says so. Peter is Peter and not Simon. Those who can accept this truth are on their way to the true Church.

* * *

Christians are often dissatisfied with their churches and pastors. In some cases, the inner turmoil of the churches has become so great that they ceased to exist.

Bear this patiently. All men defend the institutions of which they are a part, especially if they created them. God allowed His temple, every detail of which He had designed, to be destroyed. The destruction of the temple was a test revealing that His truth remains unaffected by external events, no matter how tragic. The Church will survive no matter what happens to your congregation.

My former church in Bucharest, Romania, has been bulldozed by the Communists, but I constantly receive testimonies showing that what was previously sown within its walls continues to bear fruit.

The Jews worshiped God before they had the wilderness tabernacle. Their own tents, and before this the shacks in which they lived as slaves in Egypt, served as places of worship. Our homes, too, should be churches.

As for the Church itself, why should we look so much to Christian leaders? Have you ever tried to obtain spiritual edification from the janitor of your church? Do you wonder about the propriety of such a question? Well, the Bible provides long lists of priests and singers, but then adds a list of "gatekeepers," who had "duties just like their brethren, to serve in the house of the Lord," (1 Chron. 26:12).

No history book of any other nation or religion would have included such a list. What were the names of the servants of George Washington and of the lackeys in Buckingham Palace? In what church history will you find the names of the caretakers who served in the great cathedrals?

We can learn from caretakers—and so can pastors. Wesley, on entering the pulpit one morning, said in dismay, "I am lost; I left my sermon at home."

The janitor asked him, "Do you remember at least what it was about?"

"Yes, it was about trusting God."

"Parson, trust God to help you deliver a sermon without notes." After this, Wesley never again used notes. If the pastor does not know his sermon, how will the audience learn it?

Do not look down on pastors who make but a small contribution to the advancement of the

Church. During the last two thousand years, millions of men have been educated in Christianity, but this was not the work of great preachers or exceptional pastors. By and large, the average and less than average pastors did the job. For this we should be grateful. Learn truth from them.

* * *

At the Last Supper, the Lord told His disciples that one of them was a traitor. I have witnessed such scenes often in the underground churches. On these occasions each one begins to guess which of those around him might be the evil man. But the first apostles did otherwise.

None of them thought evil of his brother. Each one, knowing the potential for betrayal that lay hidden in his own heart, asked himself, "Am I not the traitor?" Each knew his own readiness to sell even the One he loved most. Therefore the apostles each asked that most unusual question, "Lord, is it I?" (Mt. 26:22)

In my church there was a lady who always congratulated me after every sermon, adding to her praise this comment: "Your sermon was just right for Sister So-and-so." One Sunday, weary of not getting through to her, I mentioned from the pulpit that there are those who always apply the sermons to others, instead of drawing lessons for themselves. Afterwards, I was again congratulated by the same person: "A wonderful sermon! It just suited Mr. So-and-so."

Let us give up our preoccupation with looking for the speck in a brother's eye and recognize the beam in our own (Mt. 7:4).

* * *

We often meet people who appear to be perfect gentlemen. We may know of no great sin they have committed, and they may consider themselves upstanding citizens, moral in every way. But is anyone a true gentleman if he regards everyone but his own father?

God is our heavenly Father, and we owe to Him our whole life. We are guests in His world and enjoy the blessings He confers on us. We usually behave well when we are guests in another's home, but somehow we neglect to thank God for the multitude of things He gives us, and often we don't behave well among His other children.

How to worship God is not a big problem. We may express our gratitude by fulfilling the purpose for which we were created.

Is a man who does not pay his debts—assuming he is able—a gentleman? Yet Christians have a prior debt. The apostle Paul describes the state of us all when he writes, "I am a debtor both to Greeks and to barbarians, both to wise and to unwise" (Rom. 1:14). As Christians, we are all debtors who owe everyone the greatest opportunity to gain salvation. Do we fulfill this duty?

Christians must show great determination in this enterprise. If necessary, they must be willing to give their lives that others may come to a knowledge of Christ and be converted. Grateful for their own salvation, and for inner peace, and for the promise of a future life, they are concerned about the salvation of the rest of the world and look for opportunities to serve their fellows.

The world of today is not unbelieving, but ignorant. It includes the heathen, the Jews, those under Communism who are taught atheism, and those who are Christians in name only. In addition, every seventh inhabitant of the earth is a Muslim. How many of these have ever read a Bible or heard an intelligent and loving sermon? Therefore, every one of us must become a missionary.

At a Christian conference in Switzerland, an old man gave his testimony. He told how he had been on the Titanic, which went down in the north Atlantic in 1912 with some 2,200 passengers on board. Among the 700 who survived, he found himself struggling in the cold sea water trying to stay afloat.

Near him swam the American evangelist Harper, who asked him, "Are you saved? Think about your soul." With this, Harper sank under a wave of the icy sea, then after a few seconds reappeared. Again he asked, "Are you prepared to appear before the Lord?"

The man replied, "I don't know how to get saved."

"Believe in the Lord Jesus. His blood cleanses from all sins."

"These were his last words," continued the old man. "He succumbed to the rigors of the icy Atlantic. A boat then picked me up. I am Harper's last convert."

When we think about men like this evangelist, we have to be ashamed to call ourselves Christians.

* * *

The initial work of Christian missions among the Matacos and Tobas in Argentina was very difficult. For one thing, the missionaries had to walk fifty miles from their station through the jungle to get to these tribes.

One of their first converts was an Indian who had come ornamented with feathers. In his hand he had a heavy stick with which he had just killed his mother. (It was the custom to kill the dying to free them from evil spirits.) In order to obtain their magical powers, witch doctors ate firstborn children. Yet such men were converted, and some even became evangelists.

William Carey was inflamed for missionary work by reading about Captain Cooke's journeys. He asked himself, "If others can rise so much out of a spirit of adventure or in the desire to serve science, why should we not do the same in the service of Christ?"

In his cobbler shop he put a map on the wall and noted what he knew about the religions of different peoples. He constantly had on his mind the millions who are lost.

As an assistant preacher in a small Baptist community, he attended a church conference and asked whether the commandment to preach to all nations was still binding. He was not allowed to continue. He was called "a miserable enthusiast."

Later, Carey went to India where he proved to be a genius of languages. It was he who translated the New Testament into Bengali. Eventually he was to give to the people of India the New Testament in thirty-four languages.

This cobbler, Carey, became a professor of Oriental languages at the University of Calcutta. He wrote grammars and dictionaries in many Indian dialects. He was also a botanist and introduced to India many new agricultural and gardening methods. He was a creator of schools, a teacher of native evangelists.

Because of his influence, the savage habit of throwing children to crocodiles at religious festivals in Gango-Sangor ceased, as did the burning of widows and their being buried alive with their dead husbands. He also took care of lepers.

When he was on his deathbed, one of those standing in the room praised Carey. His last words were, "You have spoken about Dr. Carey. When I am gone, don't speak about Carey but about Carey's Savior." He himself chose the epitaph for his grave: "A miserable worm who appeals to Your compassion."

John Williams at the age of twenty went to preach in the islands of the Pacific. Traveling in a small ship, he went to Raratonga, the Samoa Islands, and Malaysia. Everywhere he went he brought people to Christ and established churches. Idolatry and polygamy disappeared, and many islands became sanctuaries full of the praises of God. Within a circumference of two thousand miles not one island remained without a church. In 1839 on the island of Erromanga, Williams was killed by cannibals after having brought 30,000 souls to Christ.

John Paton came in Williams' place to these volcanic islands. At first he was frightened by the bloodthirsty savages. Because of the influence of traders, they hated the whites who brought new sicknesses to their people. In their culture, a man was free to kill his wife if he no longer favored her, and the killing of children was common among them. They also believed in witchcraft. But with the gospel message Paton conquered the New Hebrides for Christ.

John Elliot, the first missionary to the American Indians in the seventeenth century, was also the first to translate the Bible into a Native American language. Thus the first Bible printed in the United States was for Native American Indians. To do so, he also gave them a written language and a grammar.

At the age of eighty he still went to visit them in the forests.

David Brainerd, his successor, went to live with Indians in their savagery, sleeping on straw in a wood hut. The Dutch colonists mocked him, but he had only one wish—to win souls for Christ.

He did win souls, but not only among the Indians. Henry Martin read his diary and said to himself, "Now I will spend my life for God." He became the pioneer missionary among Mohammedans.

In Germany Count Zinzendorf, when he was very young, stood before a picture of the crucified Jesus in the Dusseldorf Art Gallery. The picture bore the caption: "This I have done for you. What are you doing for Me?" Zinzendorf could not forget that question. He said, "A faith that does nothing is just chatter." He formed the community of Moravians, which has as its slogan, "The Saviour deserves everything." Missionaries from this community went to Greenland, to the Indians, and to the blacks.

Zinzendorf asked Sorensen, a person from his community, "Would you be willing to go to Labrador as a missionary?" Sorensen answered, "I would go tomorrow if I could get a pair of shoes." Some of the missionaries were killed by the Eskimos, but others followed. Soon the Moravians had missionary activity in twenty-eight countries.

In 1740, missionary Rauch went to the Mohican Indians. Cioop, one of his converts, later said, "First we had a preacher coming to us who told us only that there is a God. We finished with him; we had known that. Another told us, 'Don't lie, don't steal, don't get drunk.' We answered him, 'Go and tell it to the white faces. They do these things more than we do.' But then Rauch came. He spoke to us about the love of God shown in the sacrifice of Jesus, and then he went to sleep quietly in my bed, not fearing that I might kill him. So I was won for Christ."

Allen Gardiner (1794-1851) went as a missionary to Patagonia. Darwin had visited the area and believed that the Patagonians were the link uniting man and ape. They had a very low forehead, and their thoughts and habits were debased. But within two decades the missionaries changed everything. Darwin, after revisiting the country, said, "I always believed that civilizing the Japanese was the greatest miracle of history. Now I am convinced that what the missionaries have done in Patagonia by civilizing the natives is at least as wonderful." And he became one of the regular contributors to their Christian mission. Evolutionists today could follow his example!

In recounting these adventures for God, we walk on holy ground; we should take off our shoes.

We remember Henry Thomas, one of the first missionaries to Korea. While he traveled upriver in a boat, stopping here and there to preach, the natives attacked him from the shore with spears. Wounded, he jumped into the water, and in one last effort swam to shore holding up a parcel of gospels in his hand that he threw into the hands of the murderers. His wound was fatal and he drowned. Some of his attackers were converted by reading these very gospels.

We remember Bishop Hannington of Uganda who was eaten by cannibals. While he was being taken to the place of execution, he loudly repeated over and over to himself, "Love your enemies. Pray for those who wrong you. Do good to those who do you evil." When the news of his death reached Britain, two of his sons decided to go as missionaries in his place and had the privilege of baptizing and later giving holy communion to those who had eaten their father.

We think about Devasagayan, a native of India. Because he preached the gospel, he was bound to an ox and led from one village to another where the inhabitants beat him. They put around his bare neck a garland of poisonous plants that pricked the skin. Then they put pepper in his open wounds. When one person expressed compassion for the chains he had to wear, he kissed the man and said, "To me they are like beads of pearls." Devasagayan was a man who could not read, but when the passion of Christ was read to him he said, "O Lord, how bad my life has been in comparison with Yours. How can I live well when You suffer?" His last words were, "Lord Jesus, save me."

During the war, the Japanese burned alive, crucified, and disemboweled Christians, then hanged them head down. They considered Christ to be the God of the Americans. For many blacks, Jesus is the God of the whites; for Jews, He is the God of the anti-Semites; for Communists, He is the God of the capitalists. Missionaries are willing to face all these prejudices as they fulfill Christ's commandment, "Make disciples of all nations."

Strangely, missionaries have also had to fight with some of the churches. Until recently there were still American churches where blacks were not welcome. Mahatma Gandhi did not become a Christian because, being colored, he was not allowed to enter a church in South Africa.

In Romania the synod of the Orthodox church decreed during Nazi times that they would not baptize Jews. In some Lutheran churches, gypsy Christians were given holy communion in a separate cup from that of other believers.

Missionaries have to overcome difficulties created not only by their avowed enemies, but also by their churches. But it still behooves every Christian to be a missionary.

The commandment to go and teach all nations is not given only to professional missionaries. In the Scriptures, we read that it was given to men without schooling: "Now when they saw the boldness of Peter and John, and perceived that they were uneducated and untrained men, they marveled. And they realized that they had been with Jesus" (Acts 4:13). Jesus enjoined a Galilean who had just been healed of demon possession to go and proclaim the Kingdom of God.

God asks today, as He did in Isaiah 6, "Whom shall I send?" The answer is still, "Lord, send me."

Chapter 8

Proclaim the Truth

The Jewish prayer book contains the following petition: "Lord of the universe, you have commanded that we bring certain sacrifices at certain times and that the priests when they serve, and the Levites in their job, and the children of Israel, should stand in a certain place. But because of our unrighteousness, the Temple is destroyed now, the perpetual sacrifices ceased, and we have neither a priest serving, nor Levites in their office. Therefore may it be pleasant, O Lord, our God, and God of our fathers, that the words of our lips might be accepted before you as if we had brought the perpetual sacrifice and were standing on the chosen place." There is deep meaning in such a prayer.

The religious situation among Christians is in a sense similar to that of the Jews. Ideally, Christ the teacher continues His existence in the Church. St. Augustine said, "Christ and the church are one and the same person." Bossuet wrote, "The church is Jesus Christ spread out and communicated." These sayings remain valid because the treasure of truth possessed by the Church is tremendous.

But tragically much of modern theology could be called the gospel according to Pilate or according to Judas. In Communist countries many of the clergy played treacherous roles and were denouncers of their brethren.

Who are the trustworthy pastors? This is a question that Jesus asks too: "Who then is a faithful and wise servant, whom his master made ruler over his household, to give them food in due season?" (Mt. 24:45).

After putting the question, the greatest Teacher gives no answer. There is just a question mark. In the original manuscripts even the question mark is missing.

Let us also live without demanding an answer. One cannot feed his soul with questions. Know that you need good teachers in the Church. Know that they are scarce. Beware of false teachers and trust in God. The right teaching will find you. This book claims to impart it, to be an oracle of God.

* * *

The modern philosopher Bertrand Russell wrote:

"There is, to me, something a little old about the ethical values of those who think an omnipotent, omniscient, and benevolent Deity, after preparing the ground through millions of years of lifeless nebula, would consider Himself adequately rewarded by the final emergence of Hitler and Stalin and the H-bomb....

"It is clear that fundamental Christian doctrines demand a great deal of ethical perversion before they can be accepted. The world, we are told, was created by a God who is both good and omnipotent. But if, before He created the world, He foresaw all the pain and misery it would contain, He would have to be held responsible! It is not sin that causes the river to overflow its banks or the volcano to erupt. And even if this *were* true, it would make no difference.

"If I were to beget a child, knowing beforehand that this child would become a homicidal maniac, I would have to accept responsibility for causing his crimes. If God, as such, knew in advance the sins when He decided to go ahead and create man anyway....

"The usual Christian argument is that the world's suffering is a purification for sin and is therefore a good thing. This argument is, of course, only a rationalization of sadism—but in any case it is a very poor argument. I would invite any Christian to accompany me to the children's ward of any hospital, to watch the suffering endured there, and then to persist

the assertion that these children are so morally degenerate as to *deserve* what they are
undergoing.

"In order to bring himself to say this, a man
must abandon all feelings of mercy and compassion. He must, in short, make himself as
cruel as the God, in whom he believes. No man
who believes that all is for the best (in this suffering world) can keep his ethical values un-
impaired, because he will always find excuses
for pain and misery."

Because we do not have all the answers to these
questions raised by individuals like Russell, that
does not mean God does not exist, but only that we
do not understand all His doings.

Atoms existed in reality long before men knew
about them, before scientists proved the hypothesis
that postulated their existence. Atoms continue to
exist, though they still pose mysteries for us.

If we cannot explain why Hitler and Stalin existed in the creation of an omnipotent, omniscient
and benevolent Deity, neither can Bertrand Russell
explain why thousands of saints have been ready to
give their lives in suffering for love, truth, and God.

Russell has no explanation for why rivers overflow, but neither can he explain why rivers exist in
the first place and are a boon to mankind and a de-
light to the eye.

When we say God can do everything, it means He can do all things that are consonant with His character. He cannot annul the cause that produces a certain effect, though He can perform miracles. But the miracle does not cancel the laws of nature that He Himself set in motion. It introduces new elements that counteract or accelerate the predictable effects. Even God cannot make wrong thinking yield the truth.

Russell's error consists in judging reality as subject rather than object. There are beauties that can be seen only from a certain position. The position of subject versus object is not the right position to perceive and understand material and spiritual realities as they are.

One of the biblical names for God is *El Shaddai*, which means "a sufficient God." Since He answers all our needs, we don't need Him plus explanations about Him. A man can live a full life breathing air without having its qualities explained to him.

God is one, the only one. All reality exists in Him. There is no one apart from Him or co-equal with Him to affirm or deny Him. His creation, for which He alone is responsible, does not break up His oneness. "*In Him* we live and move and have our being" (Acts 17:28).

Billions of bacteria and viruses inhabit our bodies, but if they had Bertrand Russell's mind, they would deny our existence. And if they had some mystical sense of our existence, they would be against us because we sometimes take medicines that destroy them. God is far above our categories of believing or non-believing.

* * *

Some years ago while in Norway, I dreamed I heard a voice that said, "You will not always have a God." For a long time the dream troubled me, until finally I grasped its meaning. Meister Eckhardt had a similar intuition: "The man united with God has no God."

The verb "to have" does not exist in Hebrew, the language of the Bible. Even in modern Hebrew no one can say "I have money," "I have a car, " or "I have a house"; neither can one say "I have a god."

We are never intended to *have* a God. We were meant to realize our high calling by being one with God. Jesus says, "You are gods" (Jn. 10:34). We are meant to be overcomers, to whom Jesus gave this promise: "To him who overcomes I will grant to sit with Me on My throne, as I also overcame and sat down My Father on His throne" (Rev. 3:21). Only God sits on God's throne. This is also my final destination. Then evidently I will no longer *have* a God. I will be *with* God.

Everything less than becoming godlike is unworthy of a child of God. It is a shame for a prince to be only a good shoemaker.

Realize your calling and you will not ask such questions as to why rivers overflow, volcanoes erupt, children are in hospitals, and tyrants reign. You will sit on the heavenly throne from which universes are created and ruled. You will be above these things.

A good pastor is also godlike in this respect. He does not give many explanations, as God does not explain Himself much. The right pastor will help you realize your calling to be "god." You will no longer ask foolish questions. You will sit on a throne in perfect serenity, doing the right things whether you are understood or misunderstood.

* * *

The Hebrew does not have the singular "face," but only the plural "faces"—*panim*. (Every Hebrew word with *-im* at the end is a plural.)

God, too, has many faces. One of His faces is hidden, veiled in deep darkness. Those like Russell who look at that face and see nothing cannot escape the strange impulse to write against this "nothing." They are like today's astronomers who write volumes about black holes, about whose existence they can only postulate.

But this is not the only face of God. In the Bible, God is called "Our Father." The Hebrew word *av*, meaning "father," is strange. It is a masculine noun, but in the plural it receives the ending characteristic of feminine nouns and becomes *avot* instead of the normal *avim*.

So God is a father who also has female attributes. It is written, "So God created man in His own image;

in the image of God He created him," and if you ask what this image is, the explanation follows: "male and female He created them" (see Gen. 1:27). Furthermore, God compares Himself to a mother: "As one whom his mother comforts, so I will comfort you" (Is. 66:13a). Also, "Can a woman forget her nursing child, and not have compassion on the son of her womb? Surely they may forget, yet I will not forget you" (Is. 49:15).

There is no possible good that He does not embody and that, as both father and mother, He would not gladly impart to His children.

A rabbi told a joke from the pulpit: A Jew won a million dollars in a lottery. The agent who sold him the ticket asked how he knew what number to choose. "Well, this is not a problem for a Jew. In our Bible, seven is the holy number: The seventh day is Sabbath, there are seven branches in the candlestick and so on. Seven times seven is forty-eight. So I chose number 748 and won."

The agent replied, "But seven times seven is forty-nine, not forty-eight."

"Well, God knew that I was poor in arithmetic and knew I'd make a mistake, so He made 748, not 749, the winning number."

The rabbi continued, "As long as you are a member of the chosen people, you don't have to worry. God will honor even your mistakes. You will always be on the winning side." This is not simply a joke.

A few years ago, I met a prince who was a member of an Asian royal house. When young, he had decided to commit suicide. To give a genteel setting to his intentions, he looked up a radio program in the newspaper and fixed his suicide for the next day at 10 p.m. when there would be dance music.

According to the radio log, the half-hour music program was followed by preaching at 10:30. However, the man at the radio station made a mistake. At ten o'clock that night, he put on the sermon which began with the words, "Perhaps you are fed up with life and have decided to end it all. This is the right decision. Throw away your life and get another one. Jesus offers you a new, rich life." Through another person's careless mistake, the prince changed his mind and was converted.

Christians too can be quiet about their mistakes. God can use mistakes to glorify His name. He knows if we are poor in arithmetic.

* * *

The first ecumenical council of Nicea (325 A.D.) worked out a method of calculating the date for Easter Sunday for Christians . It had to depend on the Jewish Passover that was celebrated only at the time of the full moon.

However, great care was taken that it not coincide with the Jewish Passover, though the events celebrated at Easter obviously took place at that time.

Writing about the acts of the first council (which were not preserved in written form), Constantine the Great, emperor at that time, made some very good observations and some that do not bring him credit.

We read: "What could be more beautiful and festive than when a feast that instills within us the hope of immortality is celebrated by everyone without variation, in accordance with a single rite and an established order?"

But he also says: "It appeared unseemly to celebrate this holy feast together with the Jews who, having defiled their hands with an iniquitous act, have rightly been stricken as impure with blindness of soul...Your prudence would have striven in any way to see to it that our pure souls would not in any way have communicated and would not have been taken with the customs of these most worthless people."

Jesus, a Jew, was sentenced by the Jews Annas and Caiaphas, and also by Romans. We have this information from Jews whose aim it was to cause the nations to believe that Jesus was the promised Messiah. This Jew, after being crucified, was resurrected on the third day in Israel. Within weeks, the Holy Spirit fell upon a company of Jews. Thus the first church was established in Jerusalem and was constituted of at least three thousand people—all Jewish.

Why must these events be celebrated with enmity toward the Jewish people? Why must the rule demand that Easter cannot be celebrated when the Jews have their Passover—even though it commemorates another event?

The Council of Constantinople promulgated a decision in which all innovations regarding the date of the Easter feast were committed to a curse. He who in this regard "does not follow the customs of the church...as well as the impious astronomers who counteract the decrees of the holy councils, let them be cursed, separated from the church of Christ and the assemblies of the faithful."

When some Orthodox churches, under pressure from their respective governments, changed the calendar to make Easter come nearer to Passover, other Orthodox churches considered this betrayal of the faith. A split occurred that resulted in a breach of unity.

Healing of the schisms caused by hatred and discord is a consummation devoutly to be wished!

* * *

A Christian must be a valiant fighter for truth. Spurgeon said:

"When I came to London as a young minister, I knew very well that the doctrines which I preached were by no means popular, but I for that reason brought them out with all the more emphasis. What a storm was raised! I was reading the other day a tirade of abuse which was poured upon me about twenty years ago. I must have been a horridly bad fellow according to that description; but I was pleased to observe that it was not I that was bad, but the doctrines which I preached.

"I teach the same truths now; and after having preached them these four-and-twenty years or so, what can I say of the results? Why, that no man loses anything by bringing the truth right straight out.

"I wish to bear this witness, not about myself, but about the truth which I have preached. Nothing has succeeded better than preaching out boldly what I have believed, and standing to it in defiance of all opposition, and never caring a snap of the fingers whether it offended or whether it pleased."

We should imitate Spurgeon in his zeal for truth.

* * *

I have had a guardian angel for all my eighty-five years; you have also had one since you were born. What did your angel do before your birth? Angels were created long before men.

Perhaps before guarding me, my angel guarded others of former generations which means he possesses a tremendous experience of life to draw from in serving me. Our angels have the experience of the beatific vision; they see God every day (Mt. 18:10).

While in jail, I had occasion to observe fights between two groups of ants. It was always a cruel war. But if one group had one single man as its ally, he could wipe out the whole camp of the enemy with one giant step. Likewise, one angel assured the victory of the Israelites by killing 185,000 Assyrians in one night.

We possess the history of several ancient peoples, among which the most important is the history of the Jews. Many of the Jewish people were in communion with angels. Even God was called "the Angel of the Lord" when He appeared to men like Jacob and Moses.

(In my book, *In God's Underground*, I mention briefly how I got acquainted with an angel. It was an illuminating experience, figuratively and literally.)

Chapter 9

Abide in Truth

Is it ever lawful to divorce? Jesus said that Moses had permitted it only because men had hardened their hearts. A spouse who is not allowed to divorce can turn his partner's life into hell. The ideal, as expressed by Him, is that those joined by marriage should remain together for life. But where is the ideal husband, the ideal wife? People continue to have hardened hearts.

I knew the wife of a clergyman who constantly had to watch over her daughter of twelve so that her father would not assault her sexually. I advised divorce. I knew that Jesus' point of view was that of the potential victim.

Is it right to be a denunciator? Ahasuerus was a cruel despot and two of his servants had plotted to lay hands on him. Mordecai and Esther denounced the plotters to the king who had them hanged

(Esther 2:21-23). Mordecai and Esther are rightly considered examples for believers.

Not to denounce sin can be a sin. It is written, "If a person sins in hearing the utterance of an oath, and is a witness, whether he has seen or known of the matter—if he does not tell it, he bears guilt" (Lev. 5:1). This refers to a blasphemous or criminal oath.

Old Testament Joseph reported to his father the evil words of his brothers (Gen. 37:2). Someone reported to David about Absalom's plan to kill him (2 Sam. 15 and 17). St. Paul's nephew revealed a conspiracy to kill the apostle. Were these reprehensible acts?

The majority of Church fathers excuse the actions of Tamar who mated with her father-in-law, knowing that her progeny would be the proper ancestor of the future Messiah. They also excuse the incest of the daughters of Lot who did not wish to have children from idolaters; the ruse by which Jacob obtained the blessing reserved for his older brother because he knew his brother was unfit to receive it; Moses' killing of an Egyptian oppressor; Samson's suicide that killed many of the enemies of God, etc. Is it right to dissimulate (hide under a false or hidden pretense) for a good purpose?

Jansenius and Duvergier of St. Cyran, when young, decided to dedicate their lives to the reformation of the Catholic church. They also determined to keep silent about their purposes until they could insinuate themselves into high places where they would be effective. The first became an abbot, the second a bishop.

I cannot see how we can win any war without dissimulation. Underground churches in Communist and Muslim countries dissimulate constantly. Their leaders live and travel under pretended names, hide their whereabouts, mislead the authorities and secret police, and so on.

Sir Stafford Cripps, hearing one of the broadcasts of the British Psychological Warfare branch during World War II, said, "If we have to resort to this sort of thing to win the war, I'd rather we lost it." He should have seen what a lost war looks like in the shambles of Germany and Japan; then he would have changed his mind.

Other members of the British war cabinet were wiser than he. They sent an exact double of Marshal Montgomery to Gibraltar while he himself was putting the final touches to the plans for D-Day (the invasion of France). The Germans did not expect an imminent attack, knowing Montgomery to be far away on an inspection.

The British cabinet had followed a biblical pattern in which soldiers were taught to lie in wait under cover of darkness (Judg. 9:32). Ruse is an effective weapon for those who have a great calling but are weak. If anyone has scruples about dissimulation, certainly we can all agree that it is not morally necessary to disclose all one knows.

During World War II, the German ship *Graf Spee* was in Montevideo for repairs for only forty-eight hours, the time limit for a neutral harbor. Two small British ships lay in wait but were impotent to take the *Graf Spee*. The British Admiralty, aware that larger ships were too far away to arrive in time, resorted to deception and signaled that a big battleship with an aircraft carrier would join them soon. The Admiralty was sure the Germans would break the code. The result was that the German Captain Langdorff scuttled the ship and committed suicide. The British won without a battle.

Was it proper for Moses to send some Jews to spy out the land of Canaan?

Newton's laws of mechanics and Maxwell's laws of electro-dynamics are valid up to a point, but they do not work in the infrastructure of the atom. Biblical and moral laws are valid when applied correctly.

To say there exist no absolute moral laws because they do not apply everywhere at all times is wrong. This is the error of situational ethics. To say that those who apply absolute moral laws must not have concrete circumstances in view is also wrong. This is the error of the legalists. An Eskimo has to conform to other circumstances than a Zulu, which does not make either immoral per se.

Krishna taught that we should be preoccupied only with deeds, not with their fruits. Jesus said, on the other hand, that we will know the moral value of a deed by its fruits. And it is really not of primordial importance to do great works. Whatever we do, even on a small scale, should be done with a great heart. But one cannot recommend a given response for all circumstances.

There are times when we must boast and times when we must humble ourselves. When the devil comes to you with the temptation to be haughty, humble yourself because of your many sins. When he drives you to despair about your salvation, boast of your rank as a child of God.

In church confess your sin, and in every day life be a saint. Usually we do the contrary; we sin in everyday life and sing holy songs in church.

* * *

Jesus was not very polite to the Pharisees when He turned and pronounced His woes against them—especially in public. His confrontation could scarcely have pleased them. From this experience we may conclude that it is not a duty always to be polite. Politeness does not always come first. Nothing comes first *always*.

In Scripture there is a very strange expression: "it happened on the second Sabbath after the first" (Lk. 6:1). Obviously, any Sabbath can be the second after the first. Why the designation? The Greek expression is *deuteroprotos*, which means literally "the second things first."

The occasion involved the Sabbath on which Jesus' disciples did something forbidden by law. Being hungry, they plucked heads of grain on the Sabbath and ate them.

Now, there are days on which secondary things take first priority. As a general rule, filling the stomach is a secondary matter, but there are times when nagging hunger moves it into first place.

Jesus reminded those who objected that when David was hungry, he had eaten forbidden things of which it was lawful only for the priests to partake. Jesus had no word of condemnation for David, who with his small band of men had been on the run, persecuted because he defended a just cause. In effect, Jesus excused his action.

* * *

"If the law makes false suppositions," mused Mr. Bumble, a character in Dickens' *Great Expectations*, "then the law is an ass, an idiot." Laws are asses when they apply ordinary norms to exceptional circumstances.

During World War II, the Nazis wanted to deport and then kill all the Jews of Rome. The city's municipal government could not save all the Jews, but it salvaged the lives of many by changing their identities, giving them forged documents, and hiding their true parentage.

For humanitarian reasons the respective employees committed acts that would be considered immoral and would be condemned by the laws of any civilized country. But the circumstances were extraordinary and demanded extrajudicial acts. A man who really loves another is willing to do extraordinary things, even if it means breaking the rules.

We should be harmless as a dove and wise as a serpent (see Mt. 10:16), not foolish as an ass, and never mindless as a swine. (The atheist philosopher Nietzsche boasted that he was the sow mentioned by Jesus in Matthew 7:6!)

Both Judaism and Christianity have at times used questionable methods to establish their religions. Zinzendorf wrote, "If our predecessors had not used methods which our principles no longer admit, Christianity would not be. We have to thank those who did an ugly preparatory work in order that we might remain clean." There exists no ideal crystal or gas. Reality differs from laboratory formulas. So it is with morals.

Must one always speak out for the Savior? When Paul was confronted by his accusers before the governor, Felix, he did not say one word about Jesus (Acts 24:10-21). Under the circumstances, it was more important to defend himself than to witness for Jesus. (Later he did take opportunity to do so.)

Dr. Fritz, in his *Pastoral Theology*, says that it is not under all circumstances wrong or contrary to love to omit private admonition. He cites Luther's statement about the Eighth Commandment: "For when the matter is public in the light of day, there can be no slandering or false judging or testifying; as, when we now reprove the Pope and his doctrine which is publicly set forth in books and proclaimed in all the world. For where the sin is public, the reproof also must be public that everyone may learn to guard against it" (pp. 230-232).

Luther also says that false teachers are to be condemned without a hearing, without entering long discussions with them, since their errors have already been sufficiently refuted by the public confessions of the church (Walch edition, IV, 1057). And elsewhere Luther commends the holy fathers of Nicea for not allowing the Arians to defend their heresies but silencing them by "hissing unanimously."

In Dedeken's *Thesaurus*, an opinion is given regarding the question of whether public sin must first be verified before being rebuked. This is vigorously denied, with the argumentation that John the Baptist didn't ask Herod what he had done (he might have denied it); but condemned his public sin, as also Nathan did with David. Likewise Joseph told his father when there was an evil report about his brothers (Genesis 37), and Paul wrote public admonitions on the basis of what he had heard (2 Thess. 3:11). (*Thesaurus*, I, 864-865)

If moral problems are so intricate, where lies the solution? How can one know for sure what is good and what is bad?

Meister Eckhart long ago gave a reply to this question:

"Everything is good that a man does who has become one with God."

* * *

It is important to avoid quarreling. *The Fathers of the Desert* contains the story of two brethren who decided to live together. One of them said, "Whatever my brother tells me I will do." The other said, "I will always do what my brother decides." For many years they lived together harmoniously. When the enemy saw it, he tried to divide them.

One day, as they sat on a bench in front of their house, he showed himself to one as a dove and to the other as a crow. The one said, "Do you see the dove?" The other said, "It is a crow." They began to quarrel, each claiming to be right. In the end they beat each other until blood flowed, to the great joy of the enemy, and then they separated.

Three days later, distressed over their fractured relationship, they woke up to a realization of the cunning of the enemy. They reunited and lived in harmony until the end. The bird had been a swallow.

How stupid for men who worship the same Christ to fight about the manner of worshiping, especially since one's particular Christianity in most cases is due to an accident of birth.

We should also avoid slander and should abstain even from listening to it. Furthermore, if others speak evil of you, you are not permitted to reply in kind.

Michelangelo and Raphael were both great artists, but whereas the latter was very much beloved, Michelangelo felt himself despised because he was ugly as a result of an accident he had in his youth.

Once, friends came to Raphael and said, "Michelangelo is speaking much evil of you." In reply, Raphael arose and said, "As for me, I thank God for having the privilege of living in the same century as the unsurpassed artistic genius Michelangelo."

"Why do you praise him when he insults you?"

Raphael replied, "My attitude toward Michelangelo depends not upon his attitude toward me, but upon the dictates of truth and love."

Remember that not only artists, but also the workers in God's Kingdom are few. We cannot afford to discard a single one. Even if a brother is weak and a sinner, we cannot spend time on anything that would deflect us from effective work for the Kingdom.

I have no artistic talent when it comes to drawing. Once when my granddaughter, then five, saw me sketching some human faces, she said, "Grandpa, you sin. God made men beautiful. You make them look ugly." Her assessment applies not only to bad painters or to artists like Picasso, but also to those who speak evil of men.

The Bible records a notable example of the virtue of not speaking evil of another. Pilate was the sixth Roman procurator of Judea and held the office for ten years. He has been described by both Josephus and Philo as an arbitrary, tyrannical ruler who, because of this, was recalled by Rome and banished to Gaul where he died by his own hand.

We have the unflattering information about him from other sources as well; the evangelists record nothing bad about him.

The Talmud, in the treatise *Pesahim 57A*, wrote about the high priest who sentenced Jesus, "Woe over the house of Annas, woe over their curses, woe for their serpent-like hissings."

The Bible does not say one bad word about Jesus' judges.

* * *

One cannot over-emphasize the virtue of peace-making. *Mehilta,* a Jewish religious writing, says, "If in regard to stones which cannot hear or see or talk, just because they are the stones of an altar which is to make peace between Israel and their Father in Heaven, you are ordered not to lift up an iron tool upon them, how much more shall no punishment befall him who makes peace between two men, or between a man and his wife, or between two towns and nations, or between families and government."

Without peacemaking, you will never have the great Christian virtue of calmness and tranquillity. Without inner peace, it is difficult to use your time well. A Christian is a lover of peace if for no other reason than that quarrels are a great waste of time.

Euclid, the Greek mathematician of antiquity, once had a misunderstanding with a friend who threatened him by saying, "May I die if I do not avenge myself against you."

The philosopher answered, "May I die if I do not make peace with you." These words ended the quarrel.

We have a Savior who was so intent on making peace between the sinner and an offended God that He gave His life for it. We too should be willing to make this commitment.

Inner peace is a prerequisite for making peace. During a tempest at sea when the ship was tossed to and fro by the angry waves, the wife of a naval officer asked her husband, "How can you be so calm in such a storm?"

The officer drew his sword, pointed it at his wife's breast, and asked, "Why are you calm and unafraid?" Surprised, she protested, "Why should I be afraid? The sword is in the hand of my husband who loves me too much to harm me."

Her husband smiled and said, "This is the source of my calm, too. The wind and the waves are in the hands of my loving Father. Why should I be afraid?"

* * *

When Jesus preached in the Jewish synagogues, His teachings were different from the rabbis' discourses. If He were here today and were allowed in our churches, He would preach a different message from what is commonly heard in the pulpit.

When He spoke, the common people heard Him gladly, though He said things that might have been considered egocentric: "I am the bread of life. He who comes to Me shall never hunger, and he who believes in Me shall never thirst" (Jn. 6:35).

Those who took offense did so because those who had believed in Him did not act at all like men whose hunger and thirst had been satisfied. They were as anxious as ever to enjoy the things and pleasures of this world, along with miracles or high spiritual experiences no longer needed by those whose hunger has been satisfied.

May Jesus have all there is of us, as He has given us all there is of Him. St. Augustine said, "One must be very greedy to have God and to run after other things, too."

* * *

Kant testified to Jesus' ideal perfection. Hegel wrote, "He is the union of the human and the divine." Spinoza—"He is the truest symbol of heavenly wisdom." Rousseau—"He is the highest person we can possibly imagine with respect to religion, the Being without whose presence in the mind, perfect piety is impossible." Renan—"He is the most beautiful incarnation of God in the most beautiful of forms."

It is written that "when Jesus was in Jerusalem at the Passover, during the feast, many believed in His name when they saw the signs which He did. But Jesus did not believe in them" (Jn. 2:23-24—my translation from the original Greek).

May we be such ardent believers in the Perfect One that He in turn might say joyously that He believes in us because we have given Him all that is in us. I will say to men, "I believe in Jesus," and He will say in Heaven, "I believe in Richard Wurmbrand."

* * *

Many readers of this present book love Jesus, I am sure. But there are many degrees of love. The bride in Solomon's song is "lovesick" (Song 5:8). This is a sickness without recovery. You yearn for the Beloved in the same way that a person with a high fever yearns for water.

To some people, religion is rooted in fear. To others it is a do-it-or-you-will-be-damned proposition. To still others, it is social service or cultic practice. To the lovesick, it is an ardent passion that leads ultimately to being crucified with Jesus. You live no more; He lives in you. And just as His life was that of a Man of Sorrows, acquainted with grief, of a Shepherd whose primary concern was to sacrifice His life to the wolves on behalf of His sheep, so you too will take suffering consciously upon yourself.

To be God-filled, to be Christ-filled, and to be Spirit-filled, are not the same thing. The God-filled person shares God's serenity. In Him there is no variation or shadow of turning (Jas. 1:17). The Christ-filled person knows the Church is the continuation of Christ's incarnation with all the human temptations, sufferings, weaknesses, and triumphs it involves. He continues this fight. The Spirit-filled person sees his main role in being what the Spirit is—a comforter, a guide to light.

This is what I had to tell you and you can be sure these are oracles of God. Is what I gave you much too little? Is it not too big a claim to put the name divine oracles to thoughts of yours, some of which are simply common sense? You might have expected more.

Those who believe the Bible to be the oracle of God would do well to read the endless genealogies in it and Numbers 1–4 with boring details of a census. The common, the average, the boring also belong to reality and to God's truth—the more simple truths which can be helpful on the way of salvation. We should not expect things too big.

What can Einstein reveal to toddlers? What can God say to little beings like us? We are still in the primary grades, but we can get hints of what follows in high school, college, and the university.

Today's partial oracles prepare us for gradually getting the whole truth in all of its beauty.

Pastor Wurmbrand welcomes all correspondance and inquiries for current information on the persecuted Church.

U.S.A.:   The Voice of the Martyrs
                 P.O. Box 443
                 Bartlesville, OK 74005-0443

Canada: The Voice of the Martyrs
                 P.O. Box 117, Port Credit
                 Mississauga, ON, L5G 4L5

Australia: The Voice of the Martyrs
                 P.O. Box 598
                 Penrith NSW 2751

New Zealand: The Voice of the Martyrs
                 P.O. Box 69-158
                 Glendene
                 Auckland 8

England: Release International
                 P.O. Box 19
                 Bromley, Kent, BR1 1DJ

Nigeria: The Voice of the Martyrs
                 P.M.B. 21078, Ikeja
                 Lagos